Delicious, quick, to boost energ enhance well-being.

CHALLENGE CARNIVORE 28 DAYS
FOR BEGINNERS
2025

4-WEEK PLAN CARNIVORE

100 RECIPES
HIGH-PROTEIN

Copyright

VitalDietBook © Copyright 2025 — All Rights Reserved

All rights reserved. No part of this book may be copied, distributed, or transmitted in any form without prior written permission from the publisher, except for brief quotations used in critical reviews and other non-commercial uses permitted by copyright law. This includes photocopying, recording, and other electronic or mechanical methods.

Legal Disclaimer:

This book is intended to provide general information and is designed for educational and personal use only. It is not a substitute for professional advice. Any negative effects or consequences resulting from the information presented in this book are not the responsibility of the publisher or the author. Readers are advised to seek medical consultation before making any changes to their diet or lifestyle.

Liability Disclaimer:

The information contained in this book is for informational purposes only. The publisher and author have made every effort to ensure the accuracy and completeness of the information provided. However, they assume no responsibility for errors, inaccuracies, omissions, or any inconsistencies present. The dietary and lifestyle suggestions described in this book may not be suitable for everyone. Individual results may vary, and readers are encouraged to consult a qualified medical professional before starting any new diet or health program. The publisher and author disclaim any liability for any loss or damage, whether directly or indirectly caused, through the application of any information contained in this book.

Image Disclaimer:

The images of the recipes in this book are for reference only and were created using artificial intelligence. They may not fully represent the final appearance of the prepared dishes. The publisher is not responsible for any inconvenience this may cause to the reader. If in doubt, always consult a healthcare professional.

VitalDietBook Contact: info@vitaldietbook.com

Content

Copyright 2
Introduction to the "28 Day Carnivore Challenge" 5
What is the Carnivore Diet? 7
Key Principles and Benefits 7
Why a 28-Day Challenge? 7
Motivation to Stick to the Plan 8
How to Use This Book 9
How Did We Go Off Track? 10
The Unfounded Fear of Fats 10
Do We Really Need to Eat Vegetables? 11
The Power of Simplicity 11
Modern Challenges in Nutrition 11
The Nutritional Power of Meat 12
Protein: The Foundation of Health..12
Essential Nutrients in Meat 13
Meat as the Foundation of a Balanced Diet 13
The Problems with Plants: A Closer Look 14
Key Problematic Compounds in Plants 14
Example: Iceland and the Animal-Based Diet 15
Meal Organization...15
Recommended Cooking Techniques...15
Preparations for the 28-Day Carnivore Challenge......................16
Shopping List 16
What to Expect During the Challenge 18
Week 1: Initial Adaptation 19
Day 1: Starting with the Basics..20
Day 2: Increasing Variety..22
Day 3: Focused on Healthy Fats 24
Day 4: Focusing on Satiety 26
Day 5: Diversifying Textures and Flavors 28
Day 6: Enhancing the Menu with Essential Fats 30
Day 7: Celebrating Carnivore Simplicity 32
90-DAY CARNIVORE MEAL PLAN 34
Week 2: Building Habits 35
Day 8: Exploring Alternative Cuts...36
Day 9: Experimenting with Organ Meats 38
Day 10: Variety in Cooking Methods 40

Day 11: Fatty Cuts for Sustained Energy..42
Day 12: Bold Flavors and Unique Textures...44
Day 13: Incorporating Seafood..46
Day 14: Wrapping Up the Week with Premium Meats   48
Progress Test: Your Carnivore Adaptation..50
Week 3: Nutrient Optimization...51
Day 15: Discovering New Flavors..52
Day 16: Exploring Nutrient Densityl...54
Day 17: Variety and Balanced Nutrition...56
Day 18: Rediscovering Tradition..58
Day 19: Integrating Essential Nutrients...60
Day 20: Cooking with Affordable and Delicious Cuts   62
Day 21: Celebrating Carnivore Nutrition...64
Keep Moving Forward In Your Carnivore Transformation   66
Week 4: Consolidation..67
Day 22: Perfecting Techniques...68
Day 23: Blending Flavors...70
Day 24: Luxury Meats to Celebrate...72
Day 25: Complex Cuts with Advanced Techniques...............................74
Day 26: Sophisticated Dishes for the Refined Palate...........................76
Day 27: Complete Preparations..78
Day 28: Finish with Excellence..80
28-Day Carnivore Challenge Meal Plan...82
How to Use This Table?...82
Cocktails, Juices, and Smoothies...84
Cocktails..84
Juices..84
Smoothies...85
Green Smoothies...86
Refreshing Drinks..86
Conclusion and Next Steps...87
Benefits Achieved in 28 Days..87
How to Continue the Carnivore Diet...88
Monitoring and Adjustments...89
Final Conclusion...90

Introduction to the "28 Day Carnivore Challenge"

The carnivore diet may not be for everyone, but for those who choose to adopt it, the results can be profoundly transformative. If you've come here out of curiosity, a desire to improve your health, or frustration with diets that haven't worked, this book will be your ally on the journey toward a carnivore lifestyle. Here, you'll find all the essential information to make informed decisions, backed by scientific evidence, along with personal stories and success examples.

It's time to eliminate the confusion and complexity that have defined modern nutrition. Let's return to the basics: reclaim your health, transform your body, and rediscover the power of simplicity through the carnivore diet.

The idea of consuming only animal-based foods may seem radical, especially in a world that promotes a "balanced diet" rich in fruits and vegetables. However, we are here to rediscover a way of eating as old as humanity itself—one rooted in simplicity, nutrient density, and a focus on animal products. Welcome to the "Carnivore Challenge."

This book is not about following passing fads or jumping on trendy diet movements. It is an invitation to explore an approach to eating that has been forgotten amid the noise of modern nutrition advice and the processed food culture. For years, we've been told to "eat the rainbow," filling our plates with vegetables and grains. But what if the very foods considered essential for good health were actually contributing to chronic disease, inflammation, and obesity? What if the answer lies in simplifying our diet?

The carnivore diet is not just about eating meat—it's about healing. By eliminating foods that irritate our system and trigger autoimmune responses, many people have found relief from chronic conditions that conventional diets failed to address. Autoimmune disorders, digestive issues, and chronic fatigue have shown significant improvement through a nutritional approach centered on animal-based foods.

In this book, you will discover the fundamental principles of the carnivore diet and why it works for so many people. From understanding the nutritional value of foods like beef, eggs, and organ meats to analyzing how plant toxins can impact our health, we will explore how this approach is helping thousands regain their vitality.

Transitioning to a carnivore diet may seem challenging, especially because it contradicts everything we've been taught about a "balanced diet." However, by the end of this book, you will have the tools, scientific knowledge, and confidence to take the leap—whether as a temporary experiment or a radical lifestyle change. We'll guide you on how to start, what to expect during the transition, and how to personalize the diet to fit your needs and goals.

Welcome to this journey of healing, transformation, and empowerment—one bite at a time.

What is the Carnivore Diet?

The carnivore diet is a nutritional approach based on the exclusive consumption of animal-based foods. Unlike traditional diets that promote a variety of food groups, this approach focuses on simplicity, completely eliminating vegetables, grains, legumes, and sugars. Its core principle is to maximize the highly bioavailable nutrients found in meat, eggs, and animal fats while avoiding foods that may be inflammatory or harmful to health.

This lifestyle is not a recent trend but rather a return to a way of eating that our ancestors followed for thousands of years. In a world where modern diets are filled with additives, processed foods, and artificial ingredients, the carnivore diet offers a clean and nutrient-dense alternative that aligns with human biology.

Key Principles and Benefits

- **Simplicity:** Fewer foods mean fewer worries about complicated combinations or restrictions.

- **Nutrient Density:** Meat and organ meats provide a concentrated amount of essential vitamins and minerals.

- **Reduced Inflammation:** By eliminating refined carbohydrates and plant toxins, the body has a chance to heal.

- **Metabolic Stability:** Many experience improved blood sugar control, sustained energy, and weight loss.

Why a 28-Day Challenge?

The 28-day challenge is the perfect starting point to explore this lifestyle. In just four weeks, you can experience the initial benefits of the carnivore diet, such as increased mental clarity, reduced inflammation, and improved digestion. This period is also enough to overcome the initial adaptation phase, known as "keto flu," where the body learns to rely on fats and proteins as its primary energy source.

Additionally, having a defined timeframe provides a clear goal, making it easier to stay motivated and track progress. By the end of this challenge, you will have the tools and experience needed to decide whether you want to continue this lifestyle in the long run.

Motivation to Stick to the Plan

- **Health:** The carnivore diet has been shown to help alleviate conditions such as chronic fatigue, autoimmune disorders, and digestive issues.
- **Energy:** By eliminating sugar spikes and crashes, many people report stable energy levels throughout the day.
- **Weight Loss:** This diet promotes a metabolic environment that efficiently burns fat.¿A quién está dirigido este libro?

This book is for you if:

- You're looking to simplify your diet and focus on real, nutrient-dense foods.

- You want to improve your overall well-being, from digestive health to weight management.

- You feel frustrated with traditional diets that haven't delivered the results you expected.

- You want to experience a way of eating that promotes healing and wellness from the inside out.

Whether you're new to the carnivore diet or seeking practical guidance, this book will provide everything you need to succeed in this 28-day challenge.

How to Use This Book

This book has been designed to be your practical guide for the next four weeks. Inside, you will find:

- **Daily Structure:** Each day includes a clear and simple plan with specific recipes and helpful tips.

- **Delicious Recipes:** Enjoy a variety of dishes made exclusively with animal-based ingredients.

- **Useful Tips:** Learn how to overcome initial challenges, adapt to the change, and stay motivated.

By following this book, you're not just taking on a challenge—you're also learning to reconnect with a natural, effective, and transformative way of eating. Are you ready to begin this exciting journey toward better health and well-being? Let's get started!

How Did We Go Off Track?

For decades, modern diets have strayed from what truly matters for our health: nutrient density and simplicity. Instead of chasing the latest diet trends or complicating things with macronutrient calculations, going back to the fundamental principles that have sustained humans for millennia might be more beneficial. Focusing on real, nutrient-rich foods allows our bodies to thrive naturally.

The Unfounded Fear of Fats

For years, fats—especially saturated fats—have been demonized as the cause of heart disease and weight gain. However, recent research shows that the relationship between fats and heart disease is far more complex than previously thought. Some types of cholesterol even have a protective effect. This fear of fats, based on cherry-picked data and debunked theories, has led to low-fat, high-carb diets, resulting in negative health consequences such as chronic inflammation. The carnivore diet, rich in animal fats, may help reduce inflammation and improve markers like cholesterol levels and blood pressure.

Do We Really Need to Eat Vegetables?

Although vegetables have long been promoted as essential for health, they contain compounds called "antinutrients", such as oxalates and phytates, which can interfere with nutrient absorption and cause issues for people with sensitive systems. Additionally, the nutrients in vegetables are not as bioavailable as those in animal foods. For example, the iron in spinach is much harder to absorb than heme iron from red meat. For many, eliminating vegetables could be the key to feeling better and healing.

The Power of Simplicity

One of the greatest advantages of the carnivore diet is its simplicity. There is no need to count calories, follow complicated meal plans, or rely on supplements. By eliminating plant-based and processed foods, it becomes easier to identify how the body responds to nutrient-rich animal foods. Many people experience improved energy, digestion, and mental clarity when adopting this way of eating.

Modern Challenges in Nutrition

The food industry and government guidelines have played a major role in nutritional confusion. The promotion of low-fat, high-carb processed foods is not based on an unbiased analysis of human needs but rather on commercial interests. This has led to greater dependence on medication for preventable diseases and an overall unhealthier population. The carnivore diet offers a solution by simplifying nutrition and focusing on foods that truly nourish the body.

The Nutritional Power of Meat

Meat is an unparalleled source of essential nutrients that not only nourish our bodies but also enhance our health in ways that plant-based sources simply cannot match. From complete proteins to bioactive compounds, meat stands out as a key food for optimizing well-being.

Protein: The Foundation of Health

Protein is essential for muscle repair, immune function, and hormone production. Since meat contains all essential amino acids, it is a complete protein source that the body can efficiently utilize.

Essential Nutrients in Meat

- **Carnosine:** Acts as an antioxidant, protecting cells from damage and supporting muscle and metabolic health. It is found mainly in meat, making it more bioavailable than in plant sources.

- **Carnitine:** Helps transport fatty acids to the mitochondria to produce energy, promoting fat metabolism and improving cardiovascular function.

- **Creatine:** Found almost exclusively in animal-based foods, creatine enhances physical performance, strengthens muscles, and supports brain health by increasing energy in high-demand mental situations.

- **Taurine:** A key amino acid for cardiovascular and nervous system health, taurine regulates cellular calcium and improves brain and blood vessel function.

- **Zinc:** Essential for immunity, protein synthesis, and hormone production, with significantly higher bioavailability in meat than in plant sources.

- **Vitamin B12:** Crucial for energy, red blood cell formation, and nervous system health. Meat is the most reliable natural source of this vital vitamin.

- **Heme Iron:** This type of iron, found only in animal products, is easier to absorb than non-heme iron from plants, helping prevent anemia and maintain optimal energy levels.

Meat as the Foundation of a Balanced Diet

While some nutrients can be obtained from supplements or fortified foods, meat provides them in their most bioavailable and effective forms. By incorporating meat into your diet, you not only ensure a complete nutrient intake but also optimize physical and cognitive health while preventing nutritional deficiencies. This approach aligns with the goal of the 28-Day Carnivore Challenge, offering a clear, science-based guide to exploring how a meat-focused diet can transform your health.

The Problems with Plants: A Closer Look

Although plants have traditionally been considered essential for a healthy diet, they contain natural defense mechanisms, known as anti-nutrients or natural pesticides, that can negatively impact human health. These compounds, designed by plants to protect themselves from predators and environmental stress, can interfere with nutrient absorption, digestion, and even the immune system.

Key Problematic Compounds in Plants

- **Oxalates:** Found in foods like spinach, almonds, and beets. They can bind to calcium and form crystals that are difficult to eliminate, contributing to kidney stones and joint pain. They also interfere with the absorption of essential minerals such as magnesium and iron.

- **Lectins:** Present in grains, legumes, and vegetables like tomatoes and potatoes. They can damage the intestinal lining, increasing gut permeability ("leaky gut"), which may trigger inflammation and autoimmune responses.

- **Goitrogens:** Found in cruciferous vegetables such as broccoli and kale. They interfere with iodine absorption, affecting thyroid function and worsening conditions like hypothyroidism.

- **Phytic Acid:** Common in grains, legumes, and nuts. It blocks the absorption of minerals such as calcium and zinc, which can lead to long-term nutritional deficiencies.

- **Glycoalkaloids:** Toxic compounds found in nightshade vegetables like potatoes and eggplants. They can cause digestive issues and, in high doses, affect the nervous system.

- **Cyanogenic Glycosides:** Present in foods like cassava and bitter almonds. If not properly prepared, they can release cyanide, a potent toxin.

- **Protease Inhibitors:** Found in legumes and grains like soybeans. They reduce the body's ability to digest and absorb proteins, leading to bloating and digestive discomfort.

- **Flavonoids:** Although known for their antioxidant properties, in high doses, they can interfere with mineral absorption and even have pro-oxidant effects.

- **Saponins:** Found in foods like quinoa and asparagus. They can damage the intestinal lining, causing inflammation, bloating, and gas.

Example: Iceland and the Animal-Based Diet

The Icelandic population, historically living in a harsh climate unsuitable for growing plants, has thrived for generations on an animal-based diet. Rich in fish, meat, and dairy products, this diet has proven sufficient to maintain robust health and a low incidence of chronic diseases. This example challenges the idea that vegetables are essential for health.

While plants may provide some nutrients, their defensive compounds and antinutrients pose significant health risks, especially for those who consume large amounts of plant-based foods. The carnivore diet offers a clean and efficient alternative by eliminating these problematic factors, allowing the body to thrive on nutrient-dense, highly bioavailable foods. This approach reinforces the principles behind the 28-Day Carnivore Challenge, promoting a simple, effective, and biologically aligned way of eating.

Meal Organization

- **Buy in bulk:** Save time and money by purchasing larger portions of frozen or fresh meats.
- **Prepare ahead of time:** Cook extra portions to have leftovers for quick lunches or dinners.
- **Vary your protein sources:** While the diet is simple, rotating different types of meat keeps meals interesting.

Recommended Cooking Techniques

The key is to enhance the natural flavor of meats:
- **Roasting:** Ideal for larger cuts like ribs or loins.
- **Grilling:** Brings out the flavor in fatty cuts like bacon or ground beef.
- **Stewing:** Perfect for tougher cuts like brisket, which become tender with slow cooking.
- **Pan-searing:** Great for quick meals like steak or fish.

Preparations for the 28-Day Carnivore Challenge

Starting the 28-Day Carnivore Challenge requires preparation, both in meal planning and understanding what to expect during this transition. Here's everything you need to ensure a successful start.

Shopping List

Essential Meats:

The foundation of this diet is fresh, high-quality meats. Make sure to include:

- **Beef:** Cuts like ribs, ribeye, sirloin, flank steak, and ground beef.
- **Pork:** Chops, bacon, loin, and ribs.
- **Chicken:** Thighs, wings, and breasts. The skin is also important for its fat content.
- **Fish and seafood:** Salmon, tuna, sardines, shrimp, clams, and mussels. Opt for fatty fish rich in omega-3s.

Healthy Fats:

Fat intake is key in the carnivore diet. Include these options for cooking and enhancing your meals:

- **Butter** (preferably unsalted).
- **Tallow** (beef fat).
- **Duck or goose fat.**

Optional Items:

To add variety and unique nutrients, include:

- **Liver:** One of the most nutrient-dense foods.

- **Bone marrow:** Rich in collagen and healthy fats.

- **Eggs:** An excellent source of complete proteins and healthy fats.

Planning Tips

Meal Organization:

- **Buy in bulk:** Save time and money by purchasing larger portions of fresh or frozen meats.

- **Prepare ahead:** Cook extra portions to have leftovers for quick lunches or dinners.

- **Vary your proteins:** While the diet is simple, alternating different types of meat keeps meals interesting.

Recommended Cooking Methods:

The key is to enhance the natural flavor of meats:

- **Roasting:** Ideal for larger cuts like ribs or loin.

- **Grilling:** Brings out the best in fatty cuts like bacon or ground beef.

- **Stewing:** Perfect for tougher cuts like flank steak, which become tender with slow cooking.

- **Pan-searing:** Great for quick meals like steak or fish.

Avoid marinades or sauces with added sugars or carbohydrates. Instead, use melted butter, salt, and simple spices like pepper.

What to Expect During the Challenge

Initial Adaptation:

When starting the carnivore diet, your body goes through a transition period as it adapts to relying on fats and proteins as its primary energy source. During this phase, you may notice:

- **Energy changes:** You might feel more tired as your body adjusts its glycogen stores.

- **Reduced hunger:** Protein- and fat-rich meals are more satiating, which could decrease the frequency of your meals.

Possible Side Effects:

- **"Keto flu":** A set of flu-like symptoms (headache, fatigue, nausea) due to electrolyte loss. Increase your intake of salt, magnesium, and potassium to mitigate it.

- **Digestive changes:** You may experience constipation or diarrhea as your digestive system adjusts. Drinking enough water and consuming fatty cuts can help balance it.

Overcoming Challenges:

- Ensure proper hydration, especially during the first few weeks.

- Don't be afraid to consume fat; it is essential for maintaining energy.

- Get enough rest while your body adapts.

Proper preparation for this challenge will allow you to focus on enjoying the benefits of this unique diet. With a well-planned shopping list, simple cooking techniques, and an open mindset toward initial adjustments, you'll be ready to embrace the carnivore lifestyle with confidence. Let's get started!

Week 1: Initial Adaptation

The first week of the carnivore challenge is key to preparing your body and mind for this new lifestyle. The recipes are designed to be simple, accessible, and delicious, using basic ingredients that will make the transition easier while you start enjoying the benefits of an animal-based diet.

Day 1: Starting with the Basics

Motivation: Begin with simple meals rich in healthy fats to fuel your energy while your body adapts.

Meal Plan:

- **Breakfast:** Scrambled eggs with butter (3 eggs, 1 tablespoon of butter).
- **Lunch:** Beef burger with cheddar cheese and bacon.
- **Dinner:** Grilled chicken breast with crispy skin.

SCRAMBLED EGGS WITH BUTTER

- **Whisk the eggs:** Crack 3 eggs into a bowl and whisk until well combined.
- **Melt the butter:** Heat 1 tablespoon of butter in a skillet over medium-low heat.
- **Cook slowly:** Pour the eggs into the skillet and gently stir with a spatula, preventing them from drying out.
- **Season at the end:** Add salt and pepper to taste before serving.

BEEF BURGER WITH CHEESE AND BACON

Preparation:

- Shape the ground beef into a patty and season with salt.
- Cook in a hot skillet for 4-5 minutes per side.
- Cook the bacon in the same skillet until crispy.
- Place the cheese on top of the burger and cover for 1 minute to melt.
- Serve the burger with the bacon on top.

Ingredients:
- 200 g ground beef
- 2 slices cheddar cheese
- 3 strips bacon
- Salt to taste

GRILLED CHICKEN BREAST

Instructions:

• **Preheat the grill or skillet:** Make sure it is properly heated before placing the chicken to prevent sticking.

• **Pat the chicken dry:** Use a paper towel to thoroughly dry the skin of the chicken breasts. This is crucial for achieving a crispy skin.

Ingredients (for 2 servings):
- 2 bone-in, skin-on chicken breasts
- 2 tablespoons olive oil
- Salt and pepper to taste
- 1 teaspoon garlic powder
- 1 teaspoon paprika
- Fresh thyme or rosemary sprigs

• **Generously season:** Rub the chicken breasts with olive oil or ghee. Then, evenly sprinkle salt, pepper, garlic powder, and paprika over the skin.

• **Cook skin-side down first:** Place the chicken breasts on the grill or skillet with the skin side down. Cook over medium-high heat for about 5-7 minutes without moving them, until the skin is golden and crispy.

• **Flip the chicken:** Turn the chicken breasts over and slightly reduce the heat. Cook for another 5-7 minutes or until the chicken reaches an internal temperature of 165°F (74°C).

• **Add aromatics (optional):** In the last few minutes of cooking, add a sprig of thyme or rosemary to the skillet for an extra touch of flavor.

• **Rest before serving:** Let the chicken breasts rest for 3-5 minutes before slicing. This allows the juices to redistribute, making the chicken juicier.

Day 2: Increasing Variety

Motivation: Introduce different types of protein to diversify flavors and nutrients.

Meal Plan:

- **Breakfast:** Cheese omelet (3 eggs, 50 g grated cheese).
- **Lunch:** Grilled pork chop.
- **Dinner:** Butter-herb salmon

CHEESE OMELET

Ingredients:
- 3 large eggs
- 50 g grated cheese (cheddar or your preferred choice)
- Salt and pepper to taste
- 1 teaspoon of butter or coconut oil (for greasing the pan)

Procedures:
- In a bowl, beat the 3 eggs along with a pinch of salt and pepper until the mixture is smooth.
- Heat a non-stick pan over medium heat and add the butter or coconut oil.
- Pour the egg mixture into the pan, spreading it evenly.
- When the edges begin to set, sprinkle the 50 g of grated cheese evenly over the surface.
- Let it cook for a few minutes until the cheese melts and the center remains slightly runny.
- Using a spatula, fold the omelet in half and cook for an additional minute to combine the flavors.
- Serve hot and enjoy a delicious keto breakfast.

Macronutrient Percentage (approximate):
Fats: 68% | **Proteins:** 29% | **Carbohydrates:** 3%

GRILLED PORK CHOPS

Procedures:

Prepare the Pork Chops:

- Pat the pork chops dry with paper towels to remove excess moisture—this helps achieve a good sear. Rub both sides with olive oil, then season generously with salt, pepper, and your favorite spices. If desired, add chopped garlic for an extra burst of flavor.

Preheat the Grill:

- For a gas grill, preheat to medium-high heat.
- For a charcoal grill, ensure that the coals are hot and glowing before starting.

Cooking:

- Place the pork chops on the hot grill. Cook for 4 to 6 minutes per side, depending on their thickness. Use a meat thermometer to ensure the internal temperature reaches 63 °C (145 °F) for safe cooking.

Resting:

- Remove the pork chops from the grill and let them rest for 5 minutes. This resting period allows the juices to redistribute, resulting in a juicier and more flavorful dish.

Ingredients:

- 2 pork chops (preferably bone-in for enhanced flavor)
- 1 tablespoon olive oil
- 1 clove garlic, finely chopped (optional)
- Salt and pepper to taste
- Your choice of spices (e.g., paprika, cumin, rosemary, or thyme)

Macronutrient Breakdown (Approximate):

Protein: 45% | Fat: 55% | Carbohydrates: 0%

BUTTER HERB SALMON

Procedures:

- In a skillet, melt the butter over medium heat.
- Season the salmon with salt and dried dill.
- Cook the salmon for 3-4 minutes on each side until it's golden and fully cooked.
- Drizzle the butter from the skillet over the salmon when serving.
- Tip: Leave the salmon skin on during cooking to achieve a crispy texture.

Macronutrient Breakdown (approximate):

Protein: 30% | Fat: 70% | Carbohydrates: 0%

Ingredients:

- 200 g fresh salmon
- 2 tablespoons butter
- 1/2 teaspoon dried dill
- Salt, to taste

Day 3: Focused on Healthy Fats

Motivation: Increase your fat intake to stabilize your energy and satiety.

Meal Plan:

- **Breakfast:** Fried eggs with pork lard.
- **Lunch:** Beef meatballs in their own juices.
- **Dinner:** Ribeye steak with garlic butter.

Ingredients

- 2 large eggs
- 1 tablespoon of pork lard
- Salt and pepper, to taste
- **Optional:** Fresh herbs (parsley, cilantro, or chives) for garnish

Macronutrients Percentage

Carbohydrates: 0%

Protein: 18%

Fat: 82%

FRIED EGGS WITH PORK LARD

Procedures

Preheat the Pan:

- Heat a non-stick skillet over medium-low heat. This ensures that the pork lard melts slowly without burning.

Melt the Pork Lard:

- Add the pork lard to the pan and allow it to melt evenly. Tilt the pan slightly so that the melted fat completely covers the base.

Fry the Eggs:

- Carefully crack the eggs directly into the hot pan, taking care not to break the yolks. Cook them on low heat to achieve tender whites and to avoid crispy, burnt edges.

• Adjust Cooking Time:

- For runny yolks, cook for about 2-3 minutes until the whites are set and the yolks remain glossy.
- For firmer yolks, cover the pan with a lid and cook for an additional 1-2 minutes.

Season:

- Sprinkle with salt and pepper. If desired, add a handful of fresh herbs for extra flavor.

Serve:

- Serve immediately; for a keto twist, pair with avocado or spinach.

BEEF MEATBALLS IN THEIR JUICE

Procedures

- **Mixing:** In a bowl, combine the ground beef, egg, salt, and pepper until evenly mixed.
- **Forming:** Shape the mixture into meatballs.
- **Cooking:** Heat a pan over medium heat and cook the meatballs until they develop a golden-brown crust.
- **Simmering:** Pour in the bone broth and reduce the heat to low. Allow the meatballs to simmer for 10 minutes, so they absorb the flavors.
- **Finishing Touch:** For an enhanced flavor, stir in an extra tablespoon of butter into the broth just before serving.
- **Serving:** Serve the meatballs hot, drizzled with the savory broth.

Ingredients
- 300 g ground beef
- 1 egg
- Salt and pepper to taste
- 1 cup bone broth
- 1 tablespoon butter

Macronutrient
Protein: 30%
Fat: 70%
Carbohydrates: 0%

RIBEYE STEAK WITH GARLIC BUTTER

Procedures

For the Garlic Butter:

- In a bowl, combine the unsalted butter with the minced garlic, chopped parsley, lemon juice, salt, and pepper.
- Mix thoroughly until well combined.
- Shape the mixture into a log using plastic wrap and refrigerate until firm.

For the Ribeye Steak:

- Remove the steaks from the refrigerator 30 minutes before cooking to let them reach room temperature.
- Season both sides of each steak generously with coarse salt and black pepper.
- Heat a skillet or grill over high heat with olive oil or butter.
- Cook the steaks for about 3-4 minutes per side for medium-rare, avoiding frequent flipping.
- Allow the steaks to rest for 5 minutes so the juices can redistribute.
- Top each steak with a slice of garlic butter while still hot, letting it melt over the meat.

Ingredients

Ribeye Steak:
- 2 ribeye steaks
- Coarse salt and black pepper
- 2 tablespoons olive oil

Garlic Butter:
- 100 g unsalted butter
- 2 garlic cloves, minced
- 1 tablespoon fresh parsley, chopped
- Juice of ½ lemon
- Salt and pepper to taste

Macronutrient
Protein: 27%
Fat: 73%
Carbohydrates: 0%

Day 4: Focusing on Satiety

Motivation: Nutrient-dense recipes to keep you full for longer.

Meal Plan:

- **Breakfast:** Boiled eggs and bacon.
- **Lunch:** Oven-baked pork ribs.
- **Dinner:** Pan-seared white fish fillet.

Ingredients (for 2 servings):

4 medium or large eggs

- 6 slices of bacon
- Salt and pepper to taste
- **Optional**: A little fresh chopped parsley for garnish

Macronutrient:
Protein: 32%
Fat: 66%
Carbohydrates: 2%

BOILED EGGS AND BACON
Procedures:
Prepare the Boiled Eggs:

- Place the eggs in a saucepan and cover them with cold water, ensuring they are fully submerged.
- Bring the water to a boil over high heat. Once boiling, reduce the heat to medium and cook for:
- 6-7 minutes for eggs with soft yolks
- 10-12 minutes for fully set yolks
- Remove the eggs from the hot water and transfer them to a bowl filled with ice water for about 5 minutes to make peeling easier.

Prepare the Bacon:

- While the eggs cool, heat a skillet over medium heat.
- Place the bacon slices in the skillet without adding any oil (the bacon will release its own fat).
- Cook for 2-3 minutes on each side or until the bacon reaches your desired level of crispiness.
- Remove the bacon and set it on paper towels to drain any excess grease.

Assemble the Dish:

- Peel the boiled eggs and, if desired, cut them in half.
- Arrange 2 boiled eggs and 3 slices of bacon per serving on a plate.
- Season with salt, pepper, and sprinkle chopped parsley on top.

OVEN-BAKED PORK RIBS

Procedures:

• Preheat the oven to 180°C (350°F).

• Season the pork ribs with salt and thoroughly coat them with pork fat.

• Place the ribs on a baking tray fitted with a wire rack for optimal browning.

• Bake for 40–50 minutes, turning the ribs halfway through the cooking time.

• Serve hot.

Macronutrient: Protein: 35% | **Fat:** 65% | **Carbohydrates:** 0%

Ingredients:
• 400 g pork ribs
• Salt, to taste
• 1 teaspoon of pork fat (lard)

PAN-SEARED WHITE FISH FILLET

Procedures:

• **Dry the Fillets:** Pat the fish fillets dry with paper towels. This step ensures a better sear and prevents the fillets from becoming watery.

• **Season in Advance:** Season the fillets with salt, pepper, and a squeeze of lemon juice about 5-10 minutes before cooking to enhance the flavor.

• Preheat the Pan: Heat a non-stick skillet over medium heat and add the butter. Make sure the pan is hot before placing the fish in to avoid sticking.

• **Cook Skin-Side Down:** Place the fillets in the pan with the skin side down. Allow them to cook undisturbed for 3-4 minutes, which helps the skin become crispy.

• **Carefully Flip:** Use a wide spatula to gently flip the fillets and cook the other side for 2-3 minutes (depending on the thickness).

• **Aromatize:** In the last few minutes of cooking, add the minced garlic and a little extra butter to the pan. This will infuse the fish with a rich, garlicky flavor.

• **Check for Doneness:** The fish is ready when it flakes easily with a fork yet remains moist and juicy.

• **Final Touch:** Just before serving, squeeze a little more lemon juice over the fish and garnish with freshly chopped parsley. This dish pairs wonderfully with a light salad or steamed vegetables.

Ingredients:

• 2 white fish fillets (such as hake or tilapia)

• 1 tablespoon of butter

• Juice of ½ lemon

• Salt and pepper, to taste

• 1 clove garlic, minced

• Fresh parsley, chopped

Macronutrient Breakdown (Approximate):
Protein: 70%
Fat: 30%
Carbohydrates: 0%

Day 5: Diversifying Textures and Flavors

Motivation: Experiment with different textures to keep your meals interesting as you progress through the challenge.

Meal Plan:

- **Breakfast:** Poached eggs with melted butter.
- **Lunch:** Oven-roasted chicken thighs with crispy skin.
- **Dinner:** Pork loin cooked in lard.

Ingredients:
- Fresh eggs (1–2 per serving)
- Water (enough to fill a saucepan to about 7–8 cm deep)
- White vinegar (1–2 tablespoons, optional – helps the egg whites coagulate)
- Salt and pepper, to taste
- Melted butter (approximately 1 tablespoon per egg)
- Optional: Fresh herbs (such as chives, parsley, or dill) for garnish

POACHED EGGS WITH MELTED BUTTER

Procedure:
- **Prepare Water:** Fill a saucepan with enough water ($\approx$7–8 cm deep) and heat until just below boiling (small bubbles should form).
- **Add Vinegar:** Optionally stir in 1–2 tablespoons of white vinegar to help the egg whites set.
- **Crack Eggs:** Crack each egg into a small cup for easy transfer.
- **Poach Eggs:** Create a gentle whirlpool with a spoon, carefully slide in an egg, and poach for 3–4 minutes until the white is set and the yolk remains runny.
- **Drain:** Lift the egg with a slotted spoon and drain on paper towels.
- **Add Butter:** Warm the butter until melted and slightly browned, then drizzle over the eggs.
- **Garnish & Serve:** Sprinkle with salt, pepper, and optional herbs. Serve immediately.

Macronutrient Breakdown (approximate):
Protein: 20%
Fat: 80%
Carbohydrates: Negligible (close to 0%)

CRISPY SKIN BAKED CHICKEN THIGHS

Procedures:
- Preheat oven to 200°C (400°F) and line a baking tray.
- Pat the chicken dry with paper towels. In a bowl, mix oil, garlic powder, paprika, thyme, salt, and pepper.
- Thoroughly coat the thighs and place them skin-side up with space between. Bake for 35–40 minutes until the skin is golden and crispy (internal temp 74°C/165°F).
- For extra crunch, broil for 2–3 minutes, watching carefully.
- Let rest 5 minutes before serving.
- Drizzle lemon juice and garnish with fresh herbs.

Ingredients (Serves 2):
- 4 chicken thighs with skin
- 2 tbsp extra virgin olive oil or melted butter
- 1 tsp garlic powder
- 1 tsp sweet paprika
- ½ tsp dried thyme
- Salt & pepper to taste
- 1 lemon (optional)
- Fresh herbs (parsley or cilantro) for garnish

Macronutrient Breakdown:
60% **protein** | 40% **fat** | 0% **carbohydrates**

PORK LOIN IN LARD

Procedures:
- Season the pork loin with salt and pepper.
- Heat a skillet over medium-high heat and melt the pork lard.
- Cook the pork loin for 4-5 minutes per side until it develops a golden crust.
- Drizzle the melted lard over the pork before serving.
- Tip: Pair with a hot bone broth for a more comforting meal.

Ingredients:
- 200 g pork loin
- 2 tablespoons pork lard
- Salt and pepper to taste

Macronutrient Breakdown:
40% **protein** | 55% **fat** | 5% **carbohydrates**.

Day 6: Enhancing the Menu with Essential Fats

Motivation: Add fatty cuts to maintain energy levels and promote longer-lasting satiety.

Meal Plan:

- **Breakfast:** Crispy bacon with fried egg.
- **Lunch:** Additive-free pork sausages.
- **Dinner:** Oven-baked beef ribs.

CRISPY BACON WITH FRIED EGG

Procedures:

- **Prepare the Bacon:** Place the bacon slices in a cold pan. Turn the heat to medium, allowing the fat to melt gradually for even crispiness. Cook until the bacon is golden and crispy, turning occasionally. Remove and place on paper towels to drain excess fat.

- **Fry the Eggs:** In the same pan (or add olive oil/butter if needed), crack the eggs and fry over medium-low heat. Cook until the egg whites are set and the yolks remain runny, or to your preferred doneness. Season with a pinch of salt and pepper.

- **Serve:** Arrange the crispy bacon and fried eggs on a plate. For a fresh touch, add a side of greens like spinach or arugula if desired.

Ingredients:
- 4 slices of bacon
- 2 large eggs
- A pinch of salt and pepper
- Olive oil or butter

Macronutrient Percentages:

Approximately 30% **Protein** | 70% **Fat** | 0% **Carbohydrates.**

ADDITIVE-FREE PORK SAUSAGES CARNIVORE RECIPE

Ingredients:
- 4 additive-free pork sausages (100% meat, no added sugars)
- 1 tablespoon extra virgin olive oil or ghee
- 1 cup fresh spinach
- 1/2 cup sliced fresh mushrooms
- Salt and pepper, to taste
- **Optional:** 1/4 avocado for serving

Procedures:
- Heat a skillet over medium heat and add the olive oil or ghee.
- Add the pork sausages and cook until evenly browned and cooked through (approximately 8-10 minutes, depending on thickness).
- Remove the sausages and set aside. In the same skillet, sauté the mushrooms for about 4 minutes until they turn golden.
- Add the spinach to the pan and cook for 1-2 minutes until wilted, seasoning with salt and pepper.
- Plate the sausages with the sautéed vegetables. For added healthy fats and a keto boost, top with optional avocado slices.

Macronutrient Breakdown (approx.):
Protein: 30% | **Fat:** 65% | **Carbohydrates:** 5%

OVEN-BAKED BEEF RIBS

Procedures:
- Preheat your oven to 180°C (356°F).
- Evenly season the beef ribs with coarse salt.
- Place the seasoned ribs on a baking tray.
- Bake for 1 hour, flipping them halfway through the cooking time.
- For a more browned finish, increase the oven temperature during the last 10 minutes.
- Once out of the oven, brush the ribs with melted butter to enhance the flavor before serving.

Ingredients:
- 500 g beef ribs
- 1 tablespoon coarse salt
- 1 tablespoon butter

Macronutrient Percentages (Approximate):
Protein: 30% | **Fat:** 70% | **Carbohydrates:** 0%

Day 7: Celebrating Carnivore Simplicity

Motivation: Wrap up the week with recipes that embody the essence of the carnivore diet: simplicity and flavor.

Meal Plan:

- **Breakfast:** Egg omelet with chicken liver.
- **Lunch:** Grilled beef steak with bone marrow.
- **Dinner:** Pork chop with garlic butter.

Ingredients:
- 2 large eggs
- 100 g chicken liver (cleaned and free of nerves)
- 1 clove garlic, finely chopped
- 1 tablespoon chopped onion
- 1 tablespoon fresh parsley, chopped
- 1 tablespoon butter or olive oil
- Salt and pepper to taste

EGG OMELETTE WITH CHICKEN LIVER
Procedures:

- **Prepare the Liver:** Rinse the chicken liver and pat dry with paper towels. Remove any veins or nerves. In a hot pan, melt the butter (or heat olive oil) and add the garlic (and onion, if desired). Sauté until lightly browned. Add the liver and cook over medium-high heat for 2–3 minutes per side, until well-cooked yet juicy. Season with salt and pepper, then remove from heat and chop into small pieces.

- **Prepare the Eggs:** In a bowl, beat the eggs with a pinch of salt, pepper, and fresh parsley.

- **Make the Omelette:** In the same pan (clean or with a little extra butter), pour in the beaten eggs and spread evenly. When the eggs start to set but remain slightly moist on top, add the chopped liver to one half. Carefully fold the other half over the filling and cook briefly to seal.

- **Serve:** Enjoy hot, optionally accompanied by avocado or a green salad for a complete keto dish.

Macronutrient Percentages:

Approximately 30% **protein** | 68% **fat** | 2% **carbohydrates**.

GRILLED BEEF STEAK WITH BONE MARROW

Procedures:

- Season the beef steak evenly with salt.
- Cook the steak on a preheated grill or in a hot skillet for 3-4 minutes per side, achieving a perfect sear while maintaining a tender interior.
- Meanwhile, roast the bone marrow in an oven at 200°C (about 400°F) for 10 minutes until it softens.
- Once both elements are ready, use a small spoon to scoop out the marrow and gently spread it over the steak as a natural, savory butter.
- Plate immediately and savor this hearty, carnivore delight.

Macronutrient Distribution (Approximate):

Protein: 40% | **Fat:** 60% | **Carbohydrates:** 0%

Ingredients:
- 250 g beef steak
- 1 roasted bone marrow
- Salt, to taste

GARLIC BUTTER PORK CHOPS

Procedures:

- Pat the pork chops dry with paper towels and season both sides with salt and pepper.
- Heat a large skillet over medium-high heat and add the olive oil. Once hot, place the pork chops in the pan and sear for 3-4 minutes per side until nicely browned.
- Lower the heat to medium-low and continue cooking until the internal temperature reaches 63°C (145°F) for a juicy, medium finish.
- Meanwhile, in a small pan over low heat, melt the butter. Add the garlic and sauté for 1-2 minutes until fragrant, then stir in the parsley if desired.
- Let the pork chops rest for 5 minutes, then drizzle the warm garlic butter over them just before serving.

Macronutrient Percentages:

Protein: 40% | **Fat:** 55% | **Carbohydrates:** 5%

Ingredients:
- 2 pork chops (bone-in, about 2 cm thick)
- 2 tablespoons unsalted butter
- 2 garlic cloves, finely chopped
- 1 teaspoon fresh chopped parsley
- Salt and pepper, to taste
- 1 tablespoon olive oil

BONUS 90-DAY CARNIVORE MEAL PLAN

Ready to transform your health with 90 days of pure carnivore nutrition?

The **90-Day Carnivore Meal Plan** is designed to help you optimize your energy, lose fat, and strengthen your body with simple, delicious, and fully carnivore meals.

Each day is strategically planned to provide **variety, satiety, and the best benefits of the carnivore diet**, without the need to count calories or stress over meal prep.

Why is this plan perfect for you?
- **Simple and structured:** 90 days of well-organized carnivore meals, with breakfast, lunch, and dinner.
- **Variety without hassle:** From juicy meat cuts to delicious seafood, never get bored at the table.
- **Tangible results:** Increased energy, effective weight loss, reduced inflammation, and optimized digestion.
- **Science-backed approach**: Designed for metabolic adaptation, promoting ketosis and efficient fat burning.
- **Easy-to-follow guide:** Includes page references for each recipe, so you always know what to cook.

How does it work?
Our plan combines **balanced nutrition and high-quality protein selection** to ensure you get all the essential nutrients while enjoying delicious and satisfying meals.

Download your 90-Day Carnivore Meal Plan now and start your transformation today. Your best self is waiting!

Week 2: Building Habits

The second week of the challenge is all about expanding your options and experimenting with different cuts of meat and cooking methods. This is the time to solidify your habits, enjoy new textures and flavors, and optimize your nutrition.

Day 8: Exploring Alternative Cuts

Motivation: Expand your options with more affordable and flavorful cuts.

Meal Plan:

- **Breakfast:** Sautéed beef liver with butter.
- **Lunch:** Slow-cooked pork ribs.
- **Dinner:** Baked fish fillet with herbs.

SAUTÉED BEEF LIVER WITH BUTTER

Ingredients
- Beef liver, cleaned and sliced into even pieces
- Milk or water with lemon (for a 20-minute marinade)
- 1 onion, peeled and thinly sliced
- 2 garlic cloves, minced
- 2 tablespoons butter (divided)
- Salt, pepper, and a squeeze of lemon juice
- Fresh parsley (for garnish)
- **Optional:** Paprika, cumin, or herbs with a drizzle of olive oil for marinating

Procedures
- **Marinate:** Rinse and pat the liver dry, then marinate in milk or water with lemon for 20 minutes to mellow its flavor.
- **Prep:** While marinating, peel and thinly slice the onion and mince the garlic.
- **Sauté Onion:** In a pan, heat 1 tablespoon of butter over medium-high heat and sauté the onion until caramelized. Remove and set aside.
- **Cook Liver:** In the same pan, melt the remaining tablespoon of butter, add the garlic, and sear the liver for 2-3 minutes on each side until just cooked.
- **Combine:** Return the caramelized onion to the pan, season with salt, pepper, and lemon juice.
- **Serve:** Garnish with fresh parsley and pair with keto-friendly sides.

Macronutrient Breakdown

Approximately: Protein 40% | **Fat** 50% | **Carbohydrates** 10%

SLOW COOKER PORK RIBS

Procedures:
- Season the pork ribs generously with salt and rub them evenly with the pork lard.
- Place the ribs in your slow cooker.
- Cook on low heat for 6–8 hours until the meat is tender and falling off the bone.
- Serve the ribs with the natural juices released during cooking for extra flavor.
- Tip: If you don't have a slow cooker, preheat your oven to 140°C (285°F) and bake the ribs for 3 hours instead.

Ingredients:
- 500 g pork ribs
- 2 tablespoons pork lard
- Salt, to taste

Macronutrients Percentage:
Approximately 40% **protein** | 60% **fat** | 0% **carbohydrates.**

BAKED FISH FILLET WITH HERBS

Procedures:
- Preheat the oven to 400°F (200°C).
- Rinse and pat dry the fish fillets.
- In a small bowl, mix olive oil, minced garlic, lemon juice, thyme, rosemary, salt, and pepper.
- Brush the herb mixture evenly over the fish fillets.
- Place the fillets on a parchment-lined baking tray.
- Bake for 12-15 minutes, or until the fish becomes opaque and flakes easily with a fork.
- Garnish with extra lemon slices or fresh herbs if desired.

Ingredients:
- 2 fish fillets (cod, salmon, or your choice)
- 1 tbsp olive oil
- 1 garlic clove, minced
- Juice of 1 lemon
- ½ tsp dried thyme
- ½ tsp dried rosemary
- Salt and pepper, to taste

Macronutrients Percentage:
Protein: 65% | **Fat:** 30% | **Carbohydrates:** 5%

Day 9: Experimenting with Organ Meats

Motivation: Organ meats are superfoods packed with essential nutrients.

Meal Plan:

- **Breakfast:** Chicken Liver and Bacon Omelette
- **Lunch:** Beef tongue stew.
- **Dinner:** Grilled duck breast.

Ingredients:

- 100g chicken liver, cleaned and cut into small pieces
- 50g bacon, thinly sliced
- 2 large eggs
- 1 tablespoon butter or olive oil
- Salt and pepper to taste
- **Optional:** Fresh herbs (parsley or cilantro), chopped

CHICKEN LIVER AND BACON OMELETTE

Procedures:

- **Prepare the Meats:** Cook the bacon in a pan over medium heat until crisp. Remove and set aside. In the same pan, using the bacon fat, cook the chicken liver for 3-4 minutes until thoroughly cooked, then remove.
- **Mix the Eggs:** In a bowl, beat the eggs with salt and pepper. Stir in the optional fresh herbs if desired.
- **Make the Omelette:** Clean the pan (or use a new one) and heat the butter or olive oil over medium-low heat. Pour the beaten eggs into the pan, tilting it to evenly cover the surface.
- **Assemble:** When the eggs are still slightly runny, evenly distribute the cooked chicken liver and bacon over half of the omelette. Carefully fold it over and let it cook for another minute. Serve hot.

Macronutrient Breakdown:

Approximately 40% **protein** | 55% **fat** | and 5% **carbohydrates**.

BEEF TONGUE STEW

Procedures:

- In a large pot, simmer the beef tongue in water with salt over low heat for 2 hours.
- Once tender, remove the tongue and carefully peel off the outer skin.
- Slice the tongue into even pieces.
- Return the slices to a clean pot, add the bone broth, and simmer for an additional 30 minutes to allow flavors to meld.
- For an extra depth of flavor, drizzle melted butter over the stew before serving.
- Serve hot and enjoy this hearty, carnivorous dish.

Ingredients:

- 1 beef tongue (1–1.5 kg)
- 1 liter of bone broth
- Salt, to taste
- **Optional:** A drizzle of melted butter for extra richness

Macronutrient Percentages (approx.):

Protein: 40% | **Fat**: 60% | **Carb.**: 0%

GRILLED DUCK BREAST

Procedures

- Pat the duck breasts dry with paper towels. Using a sharp knife, score the fat in a diamond pattern without cutting into the meat to allow even fat rendering and crisp skin.
- Season both sides generously with sea salt and black pepper. Optionally, add fresh herbs or a keto-friendly spice mix (garlic powder, paprika, or a pinch of cumin) for an extra twist.
- Preheat the grill to medium-high and lightly oil the grates to prevent sticking.
- Place the duck breasts skin side down on the grill. Cook for 5–6 minutes until the skin turns golden and crispy.
- Flip the breasts and cook for an additional 3–4 minutes on the meat side for a medium-rare finish (use a thermometer to reach 57–62 °C).
- Remove from the grill and let rest for 5 minutes to allow the juices to redistribute before slicing.

Ingredients

- 2 duck breasts
- Sea salt and black pepper
- 1 teaspoon fresh herbs (thyme or rosemary, optional)
- Olive oil or avocado oil (for greasing the grill)

Macronutrient

Protein: 35% | **Fat:** 60% | **Carbohydrates:** 5%

Day 10: Variety in Cooking Methods

Motivation: Learn new ways to cook to maximize flavor and texture.

Meal Plan:

- **Breakfast:** Fried eggs in pork lard.
- **Lunch:** Oven-roasted beef.
- **Dinner:** Grilled salmon with crispy skin.

FRIED EGGS IN PORK LARD

Procedures:

- **Choose the right pan:** Use a non-stick skillet to prevent sticking and ensure even cooking.
- **Heat the lard:** Place the pork lard in the skillet over medium-low heat. Allow it to melt completely and coat the bottom evenly. The lard should be hot but not smoking.
- **Add the eggs:** Crack the eggs into a small bowl to avoid shells, then gently slide them into the skillet to keep their shape intact.
- **Cook:** Let the eggs cook on medium-low heat. For runny yolks, cook until the whites are fully set and opaque. For firmer yolks, cover the skillet for an extra 30–60 seconds.
- **Season:** Sprinkle salt and pepper to taste just before serving.

Ingredients:
- 2 large eggs
- 1-2 tablespoons high-quality pork lard (organic if available)
- Salt and pepper to taste

Macronutrient Breakdown (approx.):
Protein: 20% | **Fat:** 80% | **Carbohydrates:** 0%

OVEN-ROASTED BEEF

Procedures:

- Preheat your oven to 180°C (356°F).
- Season the beef evenly with coarse salt.
- Place the beef in a roasting pan and cook for 40-50 minutes, adjusting time to achieve your desired level of doneness.
- Once roasted, allow the meat to rest for 10 minutes before slicing.
- **Tip:** Drizzle the natural juices released during cooking over the sliced beef to serve as a flavorful sauce.

Ingredients:

- 700 g beef (preferably sirloin or rump cut)
- Coarse salt, to taste

Macronutrient Breakdown:

Approximately 60% **protein** | 38% **fat** | 2% **carbohydrates**

CRISPY SKIN GRILLED SALMON

Procedures:

- **Dry the Salmon:** Pat the salmon thoroughly with paper towels to remove any moisture. This step is crucial for achieving a crispy skin.
- **Preheat the Grill:** Heat your grill until it is very hot. This helps prevent the skin from sticking and promotes crispiness.
- **Oil the Surface:** Brush the salmon's skin generously with your choice of oil, or lightly grease the grill grates.
- **Grill Skin-Side Down:** Place the salmon fillets on the grill, skin-side down. Let them cook undisturbed for 4-5 minutes on medium-high heat until the skin becomes crispy.
- **Finish Cooking:** Carefully flip the fillets and grill for an additional 2-3 minutes, ensuring the center stays juicy.
- **Serve Immediately:** Garnish with lemon slices and serve with a keto-friendly side such as steamed asparagus or cauliflower mash.

Ingredients:

- 2 salmon fillets with skin
- Olive or avocado oil
- Sea salt, to taste
- Freshly ground black pepper
- Lemon slices, for serving

Macronutrient Percentages:

Protein: 40% | **Fat:** 60% | **Carbohydrates:** 0%

Day 11: Fatty Cuts for Sustained Energy

Motivation: Increase fat intake to enhance satiety and optimize your energy levels.

Meal Plan:

- **Breakfast:** Bacon with scrambled eggs.
- **Lunch:** Grilled picanha.
- **Dinner:** Pan-seared lamb chops.

Ingredients (2 servings):

- 100 g thinly sliced bacon
- 4 large eggs
- 2 tbsp butter (or clarified butter/ghee)
- Salt and pepper to taste
- **Optional:** A pinch of fresh chopped parsley for garnish

BACON WITH SCRAMBLED EGGS

Procedures:

- Place the bacon in a cold pan to help it cook evenly. Heat over medium until the bacon becomes crispy and releases its natural fat. Remove the bacon and set it on paper towels to drain excess fat.
- While the bacon cooks, whisk the eggs in a small bowl with a pinch of salt and pepper.
- Using the same pan with the bacon fat, add the butter and reduce the heat to low.
- Pour in the eggs and slowly stir with a silicone spatula, forming soft folds for a creamy texture.
- For an extra crunchy twist, you may cut the bacon into small pieces before cooking and mix some pieces into the eggs.
- Plate the creamy scrambled eggs alongside the crispy bacon and garnish with parsley if desired.

Macronutrient Percentage:

Approximately 70% **fat** | 25% **protein** | and 5% **carbohydrates.**

Ingredients:

- 1–1.5 kg picanha (beef rump cap)
- Coarse salt or kosher salt
- Freshly ground black pepper

Macronutrient Percentages:

Approximately Protein 40% | Fat 60% | Carbohydrates 0%.

GRILLED PICANHA

Procedures:

- **Select a Quality Cut:** Choose a picanha with an even, white fat cap on one side.
- **Prepare the Meat:** If the fat layer is thicker than 1 cm, trim it slightly. Make shallow, cross-shaped cuts on the fat without cutting into the meat.
- **Season Generously:** Sprinkle coarse salt and black pepper all over, ensuring both the fat and meat sides are well seasoned.
- **Preheat the Grill:** Heat your grill to medium-high using uniform coals or a gas grill.
- **Initial Searing:** Place the picanha on the grill with the fat side down. Grill for 5–7 minutes until the fat turns golden and crispy.
- **Flip & Finish:** Turn the meat and grill for another 5–7 minutes. For thicker cuts, move to indirect heat to reach an internal temperature of 55–58°C for medium-rare or 60–65°C for medium.
- **Rest Before Serving:** Remove from the grill, cover loosely with foil, and let rest for 5–10 minutes before slicing.

Ingredients

- 2 lamb chops (approximately 400 g total)
- 2 tablespoons butter
- Salt, to taste
- Dried rosemary, to taste

Macronutrient

Protein: 35% | **Fat:** 65% | **Carb.:** 0%

PAN-FRIED LAMB CHOPS

Procedures

- Season the lamb chops evenly with salt and dried rosemary.
- Heat a skillet over medium-high heat and melt the butter until sizzling.
- Place the lamb chops in the skillet and cook for 4-5 minutes on each side. The goal is to develop a rich, golden crust while sealing in the juices.
- Remove the chops from the pan and let them rest for a few minutes.
- Serve the lamb chops with the pan juices drizzled on top.
- **Tip:** Avoid overcooking to preserve the natural juiciness of the meat.

Day 12: Bold Flavors and Unique Textures

Motivation: Introduce unique cuts to further diversify your diet

Meal Plan:

- **Breakfast:** Boiled eggs with melted butter.
- **Lunch:** Oven-baked beef short ribs.
- **Dinner:** Pan-seared tuna.

BOILED EGGS WITH MELTED BUTTER

Procedure:

- **Boil the Eggs:** Place 4 eggs in a saucepan, cover with water, and bring to a boil. Let simmer for 8-10 minutes.
- **Cool and Peel:** Transfer the eggs to a bowl of cold water. Once cooled, peel the shells off and cut the eggs in half.
- **Melt the Butter:** In a small pan, melt 2 tablespoons of butter over low heat. Optionally, stir in a pinch of garlic powder or your preferred herbs.
- **Assemble and Serve:** Arrange the halved eggs on a serving plate. Drizzle the melted butter evenly over the eggs and season with salt, pepper, and a sprinkle of paprika or fresh herbs if desired.

Macronutrient Breakdown (Approximate):

Protein: 40% | **Fat:** 60% | **Carbohydrates:** 0%

Ingredients:

- 4 large eggs
- 2 tablespoons butter
- Pinch of garlic powder (optional)
- Salt and pepper to taste
- **Optional:** Paprika or fresh herbs for garnish

OVEN-BAKED BEEF SHORT RIBS

Procedures:

- Preheat your oven to 150°C. Season the beef short ribs evenly with coarse salt and place them in a baking tray.
- Roast in the preheated oven for 3 hours, turning the ribs halfway through to ensure even cooking.
- For a crispier finish, raise the temperature to 200°C during the final 15 minutes.
- Once done, remove from the oven and serve immediately with the natural juices drizzled over the top.

Ingredients:

- 500 g beef short ribs
- Coarse salt, to taste

Macronutrient Percentages:

Protein: 40% | **Fat:** 60% | **Carbohydrates:** 0%

PAN-SEARED TUNA STEAK

Procedures:

- Pat the tuna dry with paper towels to ensure a perfect sear.
- Lightly rub the steaks with olive oil, salt, and pepper. If desired, add lemon zest, garlic powder, or ginger.
- For an enhanced crust, press both sides of the tuna into a plate of sesame seeds.
- Preheat a non-stick or cast iron skillet over medium-high heat. Once hot, add olive or avocado oil, ensuring it coats the pan evenly.
- Place the tuna in the skillet and sear for 1-2 minutes per side for a medium-rare finish with a pink center. If you prefer a more well-done steak, cook for a few extra seconds without overcooking.
- Remove the tuna from the pan and let it rest for one minute to allow juices to redistribute before slicing thickly. Serve immediately.

Ingredients:

- 2 fresh tuna steaks (approx. 200g each)
- 1 tablespoon olive oil
- Sea salt and freshly ground black pepper, to taste
- **Optional:** White and black sesame seeds for a crunchy crust
- **Optional:** Lemon zest, garlic powder, or grated ginger for extra flavor

Macronutrient Percentages:

Protein: 70% | **Fat:** 30% | **Carbohydrates:** 0%

Day 13: Incorporating Seafood

Motivation: Seafood is a rich source of omega-3s and essential nutrients.

Meal Plan::

- **Breakfast:** Buttered sautéed shrimp.
- **Lunch:** Steamed mussels.
- **Dinner:** Grilled pork ribs.

STEAMED MUSSELS

Procedures:

- Rinse and scrub the mussels thoroughly under cold water, discarding any that remain open.
- Pour the bone broth into a large pot and bring it to a rapid boil over high heat.
- Add the cleaned mussels to the boiling broth, cover the pot, and steam for about 5 minutes or until the mussels open.
- Once opened, remove the mussels from the pot and serve immediately, drizzling with some of the cooking broth.
- Season with salt as desired and enjoy this fresh, protein-rich dish.

Ingredients:
- 500 g fresh mussels
- 1 cup bone broth
- Salt, to taste

Macronutrient Distribution (approximate):

Protein: 65% | **Fat:** 30% | **Carbohydrates:** 5%

BUTTER SAUTÉED SHRIMP

Procedures:

- Pat the shrimp dry with paper towels to ensure a good sear.
- Preheat a large skillet over medium-high heat and melt the butter until it starts to bubble.
- Arrange the shrimp in a single layer and sauté for 1-2 minutes per side until they turn pink and opaque.
- In the final 30 seconds, add the garlic and stir continuously to avoid burning.
- Drizzle with lemon juice and season with salt, pepper, and paprika if using. Stir briefly to combine flavors.
- Remove from heat, plate the shrimp, and garnish with fresh parsley.

Ingredients (for 2 servings):

- 250g shrimp, peeled and deveined
- 2 tbsp unsalted butter
- 2 garlic cloves, finely chopped
- 1 tbsp fresh lemon juice
- Salt and pepper, to taste
- Optional: 1/4 tsp paprika (sweet or spicy)
- Fresh parsley, chopped

Macronutrient Percentages:

Protein: 60% | Fat: 35% | Carb.: 5%

GRILLED PORK RIBS

Procedures:

- **Prepare the Ribs:** Remove the silver membrane from the backside. Rinse and thoroughly dry the ribs.
- **Seasoning:** Mix salt, pepper, garlic powder, paprika, and chili powder. Rub thoroughly or combine with marinade liquids and let ribs rest in a sealed bag for 2–4 hours.
- **Preheat the grill:** For charcoal, create an indirect heat zone; for gas, turn one burner to low.
- **Place the ribs meat-side up in the indirect zone**, cover, and cook for 2–3 hours at 250–300°F (120–150°C), turning every 45 minutes and basting occasionally. In the final 15–20 minutes, increase to medium-high heat and apply BBQ sauce for a caramelized finish.
- **Remove the ribs**, cover with foil, let rest for 10 minutes, then slice

Ingredients:

- Pork Ribs: 1.5–2 kg with plenty of meat
- Spices & Condiments: Salt, black pepper, garlic powder, sweet or smoked paprika, (optional chili powder)
- Marinade/Rub: Lemon juice, olive oil, soy sauce, Dijon mustard, or honey
- **Optional:** BBQ sauce for glazing

Macronutrient Breakdown (approx.):

- Protein: 35% | Fat: 60% | Carbohydrates: 5%

Day 14: Wrapping Up the Week with Premium Meats

Motivation: End the week with special cuts to celebrate your progress.

Meal Plan:

- **Breakfast:** Cheese and bone marrow omelet.
- **Lunch:** Grilled ribeye.
- **Dinner:** Roasted lamb leg

CHEESE & BONE MARROW OMELETTE

Procedures:

- Heat 1 tablespoon of butter in a skillet over medium heat. Add the beef marrow and cook for 2–3 minutes until lightly browned. Remove and set aside.
- In a bowl, whisk the eggs with salt, pepper, and grated cheese until evenly combined.
- In a clean skillet, melt the remaining tablespoon of butter over medium heat. Pour in the egg mixture and let it cook until the edges begin to set.
- Place the cooked beef marrow on one half of the omelette. Carefully fold the other half over the marrow.
- Allow the folded omelette to cook for an additional 1–2 minutes, ensuring the cheese melts and the flavors meld.
- Serve immediately and enjoy this rich, carnivorous delight!

Macronutrient Breakdown:

- **Approximately** 65% **fat** | 30% **protein** | 5% **carbohydrates**.

Ingredients:
- 4 eggs
- 100 g beef marrow
- 50 g grated cheese
- 2 tablespoons butter
- Salt and pepper, to taste

ROASTED LEG OF LAMB

Procedures:

- Preheat your oven to 180°C (350°F). Pat the leg of lamb dry and season generously with salt, garlic powder, and rosemary.
- Place the lamb in a roasting pan and cook for 90 minutes, basting occasionally with its natural juices to enhance moisture and flavor.
- Once roasted, remove the lamb from the oven and let it rest for 10 minutes to allow the juices to redistribute evenly.
- Slice and serve, pairing it with a light broth to balance the rich flavors of the meat.

Ingredients:

- 1 leg of lamb (approximately 1.5 kg)
- 2 tablespoons butter
- Salt, garlic powder, and rosemary to taste

Macronutrient Percentages:

Approximately 40% **protein** | 55% **fat**, and 5% **carbohydrates**.

GRILLED RIBEYE STEAK

Procedures

- Remove steaks from the fridge 30–60 minutes before cooking to reach room temperature.
- Pat dry, brush with olive oil, and season with coarse salt, black pepper, and optionally garlic or herbs. Preheat the grill on high for at least 10 minutes.
- Grill steaks 4–6 minutes per side (turn once, and rotate 45° after 2 minutes on each side for grill marks).
- Finally, cover loosely with foil and rest for 5 minutes before serving

Ingredients

- 2 ribeye steaks (approximately 300-400 g each)
- 2 tbsp olive oil
- Coarse salt and black pepper
- Optional: garlic powder, fresh rosemary, or thyme

Macronutrient Percentages

Approximately 40% **protein** | 60% **fat** | 0% **carbohydrates**.

PROGRESS TEST: YOUR CARNIVORE ADAPTATION

Congratulations! You've completed two weeks of the Carnivore Challenge. Now is a great time to pause, reflect, and evaluate how you're feeling. Answer the following questions to assess your progress.

1. Energy & Vitality
How has your energy level changed since starting the challenge?
- □ A) I have way more energy and feel amazing.
- □ B) I have a bit more energy, but I'm still adjusting.
- □ C) I haven't noticed much difference.
- □ D) I feel more tired than before.

2. Hunger & Cravings
How has your hunger and cravings changed?
- □ A) I feel full longer and have no cravings.
- □ B) I'm less hungry overall, but I still have occasional cravings.
- □ C) I haven't noticed any difference in my hunger.
- □ D) I'm constantly hungry and still craving certain foods.

3. Digestion & Gut Health
How has your digestion reacted to the carnivore diet?
- □ A) Much better: less bloating and improved digestion.
- □ B) A bit better, but I still experience mild discomfort sometimes.
- □ C) No significant changes.
- □ D) I've had ongoing digestive issues.

4. Sleep & Rest
How has your sleep quality been over the past two weeks?
- □ A) I sleep better and wake up more refreshed.
- □ B) My sleep has improved, but I still have some irregular nights.
- □ C) No noticeable difference.
- □ D) My sleep has worsened, and I feel more tired.

5. Mood & Focus
How has the carnivore diet affected your mood and mental clarity?
- □ A) I feel more positive and mentally clear.
- □ B) Slightly better, but I still experience mood swings.
- □ C) No difference in my mood or focus.
- □ D) I feel more irritable and have trouble concentrating.

WHAT DO YOUR ANSWERS MEAN?

Mostly A's: You're on the right track! Your body is adapting well, and you're already experiencing the benefits of the carnivore diet. Keep going with confidence!

Mostly B's: You're making progress, but some adjustments are still happening. Make sure to stay hydrated, eat enough fat, and get quality sleep.

Mostly C's: You haven't noticed many changes. Check if you're eating enough and ensure you're avoiding foods that might be slowing down your adaptation.

Mostly D's: You're experiencing a more difficult transition. Adjust your intake of electrolytes, fats, and rest. If symptoms persist, check the adaptation section of this book for additional strategies

Week 3: Nutrient Optimization

In this third week, the focus is on making the most of less common cuts and organ meats, which are rich in essential nutrients such as iron, vitamin B12, and collagen. These recipes will help you diversify your diet while optimizing your health and well-being.

Day 15: Discovering New Flavors

Motivation: Introducing less popular cuts is a great way to explore new flavors and gain unique nutritional benefits.

Meal Plan:

- **Breakfast:** Sautéed beef liver with butter.
- **Lunch:** Lamb kidneys in sauce.
- **Dinner:** Braised beef tongue.

SAUTÉED BEEF LIVER WITH BUTTER

Procedures

- **Prepare the Liver:** Rinse, pat dry, and optionally soak the liver in milk or water with lemon for 20 minutes to mellow the flavor.
- **Sauté Aromatics:** In a hot pan, melt 1 tablespoon of butter. Add the garlic and onion, sauté until fragrant, then remove and set aside.
- **Cook the Liver:** Add the remaining butter to the pan and cook the liver slices over medium-high heat for 1-2 minutes per side. Avoid overcooking to maintain tenderness.
- **Season and Combine:** Sprinkle with salt and pepper, then mix in the sautéed garlic and onion.
- **Serve:** Garnish with fresh parsley and serve with avocado or spinach for a nutritious, keto-friendly meal.

Ingredients

- 200g beef liver, thinly sliced
- 2 tablespoons butter
- 1 garlic clove, chopped (optional)
- 1/2 onion, julienned
- Salt and pepper to taste
- Fresh parsley (optional)

Macronutrients Percentage

Protein: 50% | **Fat:** 45% | **Carbohydrates:** 5%

LAMB KIDNEYS IN SAUCE

Procedures:

- Clean the kidneys thoroughly and cut them into small pieces.
- In a frying pan, melt the butter over medium heat.
- Sauté the kidney pieces for 5-7 minutes until they are lightly browned.
- Add the bone broth and lower the heat. Let the mixture simmer for 10 minutes.
- Season with salt and pepper to taste.
- **Tip:** If you are trying kidneys for the first time, consider adding a little extra butter to mellow the flavor.

Macronutrient Percentages:

Protein: 45% | **Fat:** 55% | **Carb.:** 0%

Ingredients:

- 300 g lamb kidneys
- 2 tablespoons butter
- 1/2 cup bone broth
- Salt and pepper to taste

BEEF TONGUE STEW

Procedures:

- Rinse the beef tongue in cold water; optionally rub with lemon or vinegar to eliminate any odor.
- Place the tongue in a large pot, cover with water, and add half an onion, 2 garlic cloves, bay leaves, and salt. Simmer over medium-high heat for 1.5–2 hours (or 40–50 minutes in a pressure cooker) until tender.
- Remove the tongue, allow it to cool slightly, then peel off the skin.
- In a large pan, heat olive oil and sauté the remaining chopped onion and garlic until golden. Add the red bell pepper and carrot; cook for 3–5 minutes.
- Stir in tomatoes (or puree), beef broth, cumin, salt, and pepper.
- Slice the tongue thinly and add back to the pan. Simmer on low heat for 20 minutes.
- Garnish with chopped parsley and serve with cauliflower mash or a fresh green salad.

Ingredients:

- 1 beef tongue
- 1 onion (divided)
- 4 garlic cloves (divided)
- 2 bay leaves
- Salt and pepper to taste
- 1 red bell pepper, sliced
- 1 carrot, thinly sliced
- 2 ripe tomatoes or 1 cup tomato puree
- 1/2 cup beef broth
- Olive oil
- A pinch of cumin
- Fresh parsley, chopped

Macronutrient Breakdown:

Protein 40% | **Fat** 30% | **Carbohydrates** 30%

Day 16: Exploring Nutrient Density1

Motivation: Animal organs are true superfoods, packed with essential vitamins and minerals.

Meal Plan:

- **Breakfast:** Fried eggs with bone marrow.
- **Lunch:** Beef heart stew.
- **Dinner:** Roasted pork tongue.

Ingredients: (2 Servings)

- 4 eggs
- 4 bone marrow bones
- Salt and pepper
- Olive oil or butter
- Optional: Fresh herbs for garnish

FRIED EGGS WITH BONE MARROW

Procedures:

- Preheat the oven to 200°C (400°F).
- Place the marrow bones on a baking tray with the marrow side up. Bake for 15-20 minutes until the marrow becomes gelatinous.
- In a skillet over medium heat, add olive oil or butter. Crack the eggs into the skillet and fry until the egg whites are set, keeping the yolks slightly runny. Season with salt and pepper.
- Arrange the baked bones and fried eggs on a plate.
- Garnish with optional fresh herbs and serve immediately.

Macronutrient Breakdown:

Protein: 30% | **Fat:** 65% | **Carbohydrates**: 5%

BEEF HEART STEW

Procedures:

- In a large pot, bring water with a pinch of salt to a boil.
- Add the beef heart pieces and boil for 20 minutes.
- Drain the water and return the heart to the pot.
- Pour in the bone broth and simmer over low heat for 1 hour.
- Season with garlic powder before serving.
- Enjoy this hearty stew that offers a firm texture and a mild flavor—ideal for diversifying your protein sources.

Macronutrient Breakdown:

Protein: 70% | **Fat:** 25% | **Carbohydrates:** 5%

Ingredients:

- 1 beef heart, cleaned and cut into pieces.
- 1 cup of bone broth.
- Salt and garlic powder to taste.

ROASTED PORK TONGUE

Procedures:

- Rinse the pork tongue under cold water. Simmer it in a pot of water with onion, garlic, bay leaves, thyme (or rosemary), and a pinch of salt for about 1 hour (or 30–40 minutes in a pressure cooker) until tender. Cool slightly and peel off the skin.
- Preheat the oven to 200°C (390°F). Either slice the tongue thickly or leave it whole. In a bowl, mix olive oil, salt, pepper, your chosen spices, and optional lemon juice; then coat the tongue evenly. Place it in a baking tray with a splash of broth to prevent drying and roast for 20–25 minutes, turning halfway.
- Alternatively, if grilling, remove the meat from the grill, loosely cover with foil, and let it rest for 5 minutes before serving with your favorite sides.

Macronutrients:

Approximately 35% **protein** | 60% **fat** | 5% **carbohydrates.**

Ingredients:

- 1 pork tongue 500g
- 1 medium onion, peeled and quartered
- 2 garlic cloves
- 2 bay leaves
- 1 sprig of thyme or rosemary
- Salt and pepper, to taste
- Olive oil
- Preferred spices (paprika, cumin, etc.)
- Juice of 1 lemon (optional)
- 1 cup broth

Day 17: Variety and Balanced Nutrition

Motivation: Incorporate collagen-rich cuts to support joint and skin health.

Meal Plan:

- **Breakfast:** Crispy bacon with scrambled eggs.
- **Lunch:** Pork trotters in their own juice.
- **Dinner:** Braised oxtail.

Ingredients:
- 4 slices of bacon
- 4 eggs
- 2 tsp heavy cream
- 1 tsp butter
- Salt and pepper to taste
- **Optional:** fresh herbs, avocado slices, or sautéed spinach

CRISPY BACON WITH SCRAMBLED EGGS

Instructions:

- **Cook the Bacon:** Heat a skillet over medium heat. Cook the bacon for 2-3 minutes per side until crispy. Remove and place on a paper towel to drain excess grease.
- **Prepare the Eggs:** In a bowl, whisk the eggs with salt, pepper, and heavy cream.
- **Cook the Eggs:** In the same skillet, melt the butter over low heat. Pour in the eggs and stir gently until they reach a soft, creamy texture.
- **Serve:** Plate the scrambled eggs with the crispy bacon. Garnish with fresh herbs or serve with avocado slices or sautéed spinach for an extra nutrient boost.

Macronutrient Breakdown:

Fat: 75% | **Protein:** 25% | **Carbohydrates:** 0% (trace amounts from optional ingredients)

OXTAIL STEW

Instructions:

- Heat a pot over medium-high heat. Sear the oxtail on all sides until golden brown.
- Pour in the bone broth, ensuring the meat is fully submerged.
- Lower the heat to a gentle simmer and cover. Cook for 4–5 hours until the meat is tender and falls off the bone.
- Season with salt and pepper to taste.
- Serve hot, enjoying the rich, collagen-packed broth.

Ingredients:

- 500 g (1.1 lbs) oxtail
- 1 liter (4 cups) bone broth
- Salt and pepper to taste

Macronutrient Ratio:

Fat: 70% | **Protein:** 30% | **Carbohydrates:** 0%

PIG TROTTERS IN THEIR OWN JUICE

Instructions:

- **Cook the Trotters:** Rinse the pig trotters well. Place them in a pot with water, onion, two garlic cloves, bay leaves, thyme, and salt. Simmer for 1.5-2 hours or 40-50 minutes in a pressure cooker until tender.
- **Prepare the Sauce:** Roast the tomatoes until charred. Blend with soaked chilies, cumin, oregano, and remaining garlic. Add soaking water if needed. Blend until smooth.
- **Sauté the Sauce:** Heat oil in a large pan. Fry the sauce for 5-7 minutes,stirring constantly. Add broth or water, seasoning with salt and pepper.
- **Combine & Simmer:** Add the cooked trotters to the sauce. Simmer for 20-30 minutes to absorb flavors.
- **Serve:** Serve hot in a bowl with its broth.

Ingredients:

- 4 pig trotters, halved, cleaned
- 1 large onion, quartered
- 4 garlic cloves
- 3 bay leaves
- 1 sprig fresh thyme
- 1 sprig fresh parsley
- 2 guajillo chilies (seeded, soaked)
- 2 ancho chilies (seeded, soaked)
- 1 tsp ground cumin
- 1 tsp dried oregano
- 2 large tomatoes, roasted
- 1 liter beef or chicken broth (or water)
- Salt and pepper to taste
- Cooking oil

Macronutrient Breakdown:

Fats: 70% | **Protein:** 25% | **Carbs:** 5%

Day 18: Rediscovering Tradition

Motivation: Less common cuts have been staples in traditional cooking and offer an impressive nutritional profile.

Meal Plan:

- **Breakfast:** Omelet with chicken liver.
- **Lunch:** Oven-roasted lamb shank.
- **Dinner:** Pan-seared kidneys with garlic.

Ingredients

- 150 g chicken liver, cleaned and chopped
- 4 large eggs
- 1/4 cup heavy cream (optional, for creamier texture)
- 1/4 onion, finely chopped
- 1 garlic clove, minced
- 2 tbsp butter or olive oil
- Salt and pepper to taste
- **Optional:** fresh herbs (parsley or chives) for garnish

CHICKEN LIVER OMELETTE

Instructions

- Prep the Liver: Soak the chicken liver in milk or water with a splash of vinegar for 20-30 minutes to reduce its strong taste. Pat dry with paper towels.

- Sauté the Liver: Heat 1 tbsp butter in a pan. Sauté the onion and garlic until golden. Add the liver and cook for 5-7 minutes until browned and fully cooked. Season with salt and pepper. Set aside.

- Cook the Omelette: Whisk eggs with heavy cream and a pinch of salt. Melt the remaining butter in a clean pan over medium-low heat. Pour in the eggs, tilting the pan to spread evenly.

- Assemble: Once the edges set but the center is slightly moist, add the liver. Fold the omelette and cook for 1 more minute. Serve hot, garnished with herbs.

Macronutrient Ratio:

Fat: 70% | **Protein:** 25% | **Carbs:** 5%

ROASTED LAMB LEG

Instructions:

- Preheat the oven to 180°C (350°F).
- Rub the lamb leg with salt, rosemary, and garlic powder.
- Place it in a baking tray and bake for 90 minutes, turning it halfway through.
- For a crispier texture, increase the temperature to 220°C (430°F) for the last 10 minutes.
- Serve with its own cooking juices.

Ingredients:

- 1 lamb leg (approximately 1 kg)
- 2 tbsp butter
- Salt, rosemary, and garlic powder to taste

Macronutrient Breakdown (per serving, assuming 2 servings):

Fat: 70% | **Protein:** 30% | **Carb.:** 0%

PAN-SEARED KIDNEYS WITH GARLIC

Instructions:

- **Clean the Kidneys:** Slice the kidneys in half and remove any fat or white membranes. Rinse under cold water. For a milder taste, soak them in salted water with a few drops of vinegar or lemon juice for 30 minutes, then drain.
- **Preparation:** Cut the kidneys into thin slices or bite-sized pieces. Pat them dry with paper towels to remove excess moisture.
- **Cooking:** Heat butter and olive oil in a large skillet over medium heat. Add the minced garlic and sauté until golden but not burnt.
- **Sear the Kidneys**: Add the kidney slices and cook for 5-7 minutes, stirring occasionally until browned on the outside and tender inside. Avoid overcooking to prevent toughness.
- **Final Touch:** Season with salt, pepper, and a squeeze of lemon juice. Sprinkle fresh parsley for added flavor.
- **Serving:** Serve hot with a keto-friendly side like mashed cauliflower or sautéed asparagus.

Ingredients:

- 400g beef or pork kidneys
- 4 garlic cloves, minced
- 2 tbsp butter
- 1 tbsp extra virgin olive oil
- 1 tsp fresh parsley, finely chopped
- Salt and pepper to taste
- 1 tsp lemon juice

Macronutrient Breakdown:

Fats: 70% | Proteins: 25% | Carb.: 5%

Day 19: Integrating Essential Nutrients

Motivation: Organs are a rich source of B vitamins, iron, and other nutrients that are hard to find in other foods.

Meal Plan:

- **Breakfast:** Eggs with duck liver.
- **Lunch:** Sautéed brains with butter.
- **Dinner:** Oven-baked pork ribs.

Ingredients (2 servings):

- 2 pieces of duck liver (about 200 g total)
- 4 large eggs
- 2 tbsp butter or ghee
- 1 garlic clove, finely chopped
- 1 tsp fresh parsley, chopped (optional)
- Salt and pepper to taste
- Spinach leaves or avocado slices for serving (optional)

DUCK LIVER AND EGGS

Instructions:

- **Prepare the Duck Liver:** Pat dry with a paper towel and season with salt and pepper.

- **Cook the Liver:** Heat 1 tbsp butter or ghee in a pan over medium heat. Add garlic and sauté for 30 seconds. Place the liver in the pan, cooking 2-3 minutes per side until browned but tender inside. Avoid overcooking. Remove and set aside.

- **Cook the Eggs:** In the same pan, add the remaining butter or ghee. Crack the eggs directly into the pan and cook as desired (fried, scrambled, or poached). Season with salt and pepper.

- **Serve:** Plate the duck liver and eggs, garnishing with parsley. Optionally, serve with sautéed spinach or avocado slices.

Macronutrient Breakdown:

Fat: 70% | **Protein:** 25% | **Carbs:** 5%

SAUTÉED BRAIN WITH BUTTER

Instructions:

- Rinse the brain thoroughly and remove any membranes. Cut it into small pieces.
- Heat a skillet over medium heat and melt the butter.
- Add the brain pieces and cook for about 5 minutes, stirring occasionally.
- Season with salt to taste.
- Serve hot, optionally with a light broth to enhance the flavors.

Macronutrient Breakdown:

Fat: 70% Protein: 25% Carbs: 5%

- **Ingredients:**
- 200 g brain (beef or pork)
- 2 tbsp butter
- Salt to taste

OVEN-BAKED PORK RIBS

Instructions:

- Preheat the oven to 160°C (320°F). Low temperature ensures tender ribs.
- Prepare the ribs by removing the membrane from the back to enhance flavor absorption.
- Season the ribs by mixing olive oil, garlic, paprika, oregano, cumin, salt, and pepper. Rub the mixture generously over the meat.
- Wrap and bake: Place ribs bone-side down on a baking tray, cover tightly with foil, and bake for 2-3 hours until tender.
- Glaze and broil (optional): Increase the temperature to 200°C (390°F), remove the foil, brush with BBQ sauce, and broil for 10-15 minutes until caramelized.
- Rest & serve: Let the ribs rest for 5-10 minutes before slicing.

Macronutrient Breakdown (Approximate):

Fat: 70% | Protein: 28% | Carbs: 2% (if using BBQ sauce)

Ingredients:

- 1 rack of pork ribs (about 1 kg)
- 2 tbsp olive oil
- 2 garlic cloves, minced
- 1 tsp smoked paprika
- 1 tsp oregano
- 1 tsp ground cumin
- Salt and pepper to taste
- ½ cup BBQ sauce (optional, for glazing)

Day 20: Cooking with Affordable and Delicious Cuts

Motivation: Learn how to use lesser-known cuts that are both delicious and budget-friendly.

Meal Plan:

- **Breakfast:** Bacon with bone marrow.
- **Lunch:** Braised pork ear.
- **Dinner:** Roasted lamb tongue.

Ingredients (2 servings):
- 4 slices of high-quality bacon
- 2 beef marrow bones, split lengthwise
- Salt and pepper to taste
- Optional: Fresh parsley, chopped

BACON WITH BONE MARROW

Instructions:

- **Preheat the Oven:** Set your oven to 200°C (390°F). Place marrow bones on a baking tray, cut side up. Season with salt and pepper.
- **Roast the Marrow:** Bake for 15-20 minutes until the marrow is hot and slightly golden. Avoid overcooking to maintain a creamy texture.
- **Cook the Bacon:** While the marrow roasts, heat a skillet over medium heat and cook the bacon until crispy. Drain excess fat if desired.
- **Serve:** Plate the bacon with the hot marrow bones. Optionally, garnish with fresh parsley.
- **Enjoy:** Scoop the marrow onto the crispy bacon or eat it directly from the bone.

Macronutrient Breakdown:

Fat: 75% | **Protein:** 24% | **Carbs:** 1%

BRAISED PORK EARS STEW

Instructions:

- Prepare the pork ears: Rinse them well under cold water and remove any excess fat.
- For a softer texture, boil them in salted water for 15-20 minutes, then drain and slice into strips.
- Make the sofrito: Heat olive oil in a pan over medium heat. Sauté the onion, garlic, and bell pepper until softened.
- Add the tomatoes and spices: Stir in crushed tomatoes, sweet paprika, and spicy paprika. Cook for 5 minutes, stirring.
- Incorporate the pork ears: Mix in the sliced pork ears, ensuring they absorb the flavors.
- Deglaze and braise: Pour in the white wine and let the alcohol evaporate for 2-3 minutes.
- Add broth, bay leaf, salt, and pepper. Simmer on low heat for 30-40 minutes until tender.
- Adjust and serve: Taste and adjust seasoning. Serve hot, optionally garnished with parsley.

Ingredients:
- 2 pork ears
- 1 medium onion, chopped
- 2 garlic cloves, minced
- 1 red bell pepper, sliced
- 200 g crushed tomatoes
- 1/2 cup white wine
- 500 ml beef broth or water
- 1 tsp sweet paprika
- 1/2 tsp spicy paprika (optional)
- 1 bay leaf
- Olive oil
- Salt and pepper to taste

Macronutrient Breakdown:

Fats: 70% | **Proteins:** 25% | **Carbohydrates:** 5%

ROASTED LAMB TONGUE

Instructions:
- Preheat the oven to 350°F (180°C).
- Rinse the lamb tongues thoroughly under cold water.
- Pat dry with a paper towel and season evenly with salt and garlic powder.
- Place the tongues on a baking sheet or in an oven-safe dish.
- Roast for 30-40 minutes, or until the tongues are tender and slightly browned.
- Remove from the oven and let rest for a few minutes before slicing.
- Serve with the natural juices for added flavor.

Ingredients:
- 2 lamb tongues
- Salt, to taste
- Garlic powder, to taste

Macronutrient Breakdown: **Fat:** 70% | **Protein:** 30% | **Carbs:** 0%

Day 21: Celebrating Carnivore Nutrition

Motivation: Finish this week with nutrient-dense recipes that strengthen your body.

Meal Plan:

- **Breakfast:** Omelet with liver and cheese.
- **Lunch:** Braised oxtail stew.
- **Dinner:** Garlic lamb kidneys.

Ingredients (Serves 2):

- 2 large eggs
- 100 g beef or chicken liver (chicken liver has a milder taste)
- 50 g shredded cheese (cheddar, gouda, or mozzarella)
- ¼ small onion (optional, finely chopped)
- 1 garlic clove (minced)
- 2 tbsp butter or coconut oil
- Salt and pepper to taste
- Fresh herbs (parsley or cilantro, optional)

PANCETTA WITH BONE MARROW OMELET

Instructions:

- **Prepare the liver:** Trim any membranes and cut into small pieces. Season with salt and pepper.

- **Cook the liver:** Heat 1 tbsp butter in a pan over medium heat. Sauté garlic and onion until soft. Add liver and cook for 3-4 minutes until browned. Set aside.

- **Beat the eggs:** In a bowl, whisk eggs with salt and pepper.

- **Cook the omelet:** In the same pan, melt the remaining butter. Pour in eggs and cook for 1-2 minutes until slightly set.

- **Fill the omelet:** Add liver and cheese to one side. Fold over and cook 1 more minute until cheese melts.

- **Serve:** Garnish with fresh herbs if desired.

Macronutrient Ratio:

Fat: 70% | **Protein:** 25% | **Carbs:** 5%

OXTAIL STEW (CARNIVORE STYLE)

Instructions:

- Heat a pot over medium-high heat. Sear the oxtail on all sides until browned.
- Pour in the bone broth and bring to a gentle simmer.
- Reduce heat to low, cover, and cook for 4 hours until the meat is tender and falls off the bone.
- Season with salt and pepper to taste.
- Serve hot.
- **Tip:** Use the leftover broth for a nourishing soup the next day.

Ingredients:

- 500 g (1.1 lbs) oxtail
- 2 cups bone broth
- Salt and pepper to taste

Macronutrient Ratio:

Fat: 70% Protein: 30% Carbs: 0%

GARLIC LAMB KIDNEYS

Instructions:

- **Prepare the Kidneys:** Rinse the kidneys under cold water. Remove the white membrane and inner ducts. Soak in water with vinegar or lemon juice for 30 minutes. Rinse and pat dry.
- **Sauté the Garlic:** Heat butter and olive oil in a skillet over medium-high heat. Add garlic and sauté until lightly golden, without burning.
- **Cook the Kidneys:** Add the chopped kidneys to the skillet. Stir-fry for 3-5 minutes, ensuring even cooking. Season with salt, pepper, and optional paprika.
- **Finish with Lemon and Herbs:** Once golden, pour in lemon juice and sprinkle with parsley. Cook for 1 more minute to blend flavors.
- **Serve Hot:** Enjoy with keto-friendly sides like cauliflower mash, grilled asparagus, or a fresh salad.

Ingredients:

- 300 g lamb kidneys (cleaned and chopped)
- 4 garlic cloves (finely chopped)
- 2 tbsp butter
- 1 tbsp olive oil
- 1 tsp paprika (optional)
- 1 tbsp fresh parsley (chopped)
- Juice of 1/2 lemon
- Salt and pepper to taste

Macronutrient Breakdown:

Fat: 70% | **Protein:** 25% | **Carbs:** 5%

KEEP MOVING FORWARD IN YOUR CARNIVORE TRANSFORMATION

You've already completed three weeks of the Carnivore Challenge: 28 Days! You're on the right track, and with each passing day, your body continues to adapt and reap the benefits of the carnivore diet.

But this is just the beginning. There's still one more week to go in this challenge, and beyond that, many more opportunities to keep learning and optimizing your health.

DISCOVER MORE AT VITAL DIET BOOK

If you're enjoying this challenge and want to dive deeper into the carnivore diet and other nutritional strategies, I invite you to explore more content at **vitaldietbook.com**.

I'll soon be publishing new books, recipes, and exclusive resources to help you take your health to the next level. Scan the QR code below to explore more and stay on track toward a stronger, healthier life

THANK YOU FOR BEING PART OF THIS JOURNEY

Your commitment and dedication are the keys to your success. I'm excited to support you in this process and continue providing you with valuable insights and tools to help you reach your goals.

Stay strong, stay carnivore, and keep going. The best is yet to come!

Week 4: Consolidation

The final week of the 28-Day Carnivore Challenge is designed to solidify your habits and explore more advanced recipes that will help you master this lifestyle. At this stage, you will have experienced the benefits of the carnivore diet and will be ready to incorporate techniques and flavors that enhance your experience.

Day 22: Perfecting Techniques

Motivation: Elevate your cooking skills with techniques that enhance the natural flavors of meat.

Meal Plan:

- **Breakfast:** Eggs Benedict with clarified butter.
- **Lunch:** Oven-roasted prime rib.
- **Dinner:** Pork chops with bone marrow sauce.

CARNIVORE EGGS BENEDICT WITH BUTTER

Ingredients:
- 2 fresh eggs
- 2 slices of avocado
- 2 slices of ham or bacon
- 2 tbsp white vinegar
- 50 g clarified butter (ghee)
- Salt and pepper to taste

Instructions:

- **Poach the Eggs:** Heat a pot of water until nearly boiling. Add vinegar. Crack an egg into a small bowl. Swirl the water to create a vortex and gently drop the egg in. Cook for 3–4 minutes for a runny yolk. Repeat with the second egg. Remove with a slotted spoon and drain on paper towels.

- **Prepare the Butter:** Melt the ghee over low heat until fully liquid and warm.

- **Assemble the Eggs Benedict:** Place avocado slices as the base (or omit for strict carnivore). Layer with ham or bacon. Top with the poached egg. Drizzle generously with warm clarified butter.

- **Final Touches:** Season with salt and pepper. Garnish with a sprinkle of smoked paprika (optional).

Macronutrient Breakdown:

Fat: 75% | **Protein:** 23% | **Carbs:** 2% (from avocado, optional)

PRIME RIB ROAST

Instructions:

- Preheat the oven to 180°C (350°F).
- Season the prime rib generously with coarse salt and rub it with softened butter.
- Roast for 60–90 minutes, depending on your preferred doneness:
- Rare: 50°C (122°F)
- Medium-rare: 55°C (131°F)
- Medium: 60°C (140°F)
- Rest the meat for 10 minutes before slicing to preserve its juices.
- **Tip:** Use a meat thermometer for precision.

Ingredients:

- 1 kg (2.2 lbs) prime rib (beef rib roast)
- 2 tbsp butter
- Coarse salt, to taste

Macronutrient Breakdown (per serving)

Fat: 70% | **Protein:** 30% | **Carbs:** 0%

PORK CHOPS WITH BONE MARROW SAUCE

Instructions:

- **Prepare the Pork Chops:** Season the chops with salt and pepper. Heat butter in a skillet over medium-high heat. Cook the pork chops for 4-5 minutes per side until golden and reach 145°F (63°C). Remove from heat and let them rest under foil.
- **Make the Bone Marrow Sauce:** In the same skillet, sauté garlic until fragrant (1 minute). Place the bone marrow halves cut-side down and cook for 3-4 minutes until slightly melted.
- **Finish the Sauce:** Pour in the beef broth, scraping the pan to deglaze. Stir in the heavy cream and thyme, cooking for 3-5 minutes until the sauce thickens. Use a fork to scoop out the marrow and mix it in.
- **Serve:** Drizzle the sauce over the pork chops, garnish with parsley, and finish with a drizzle of olive oil.

Ingredients:
- 2 pork chops
- 1 tbsp butter
- Salt and pepper, to taste
- 1 garlic clove, minced
- 100 ml beef broth
- 2 bone marrow pieces, halved
- 1 tbsp heavy cream
- 1 tbsp olive oil
- ½ tsp thyme
- ½ tsp fresh parsley, chopped (for garnish)

Macronutrient Ratio:

Fat: 70% | **Protein:** 25% | **Carbs:** 5%

Day 23: Blending Flavors

Motivation: Experiment with simple combinations that highlight the richness of fats and proteins.

Meal Plan:

- **Breakfast:** Crispy bacon with bone marrow.
- **Lunch:** Lamb stew with butter.
- **Dinner:** Grilled red mullet with garlic.

CRISPY BACON WITH BONE MARROW

Instructions:

- **Roast the marrow:** Preheat the oven to 200°C (390°F). Place the bones on a baking tray, cut side up. Roast for 15-20 minutes until the marrow is soft and bubbling. Avoid overcooking to maintain a creamy texture.

- **Cook the bacon:** Heat a pan over medium heat. Cook the bacon strips for 3-4 minutes per side until golden and crispy. Remove and let drain on paper towels.

- **Serve:** Place the roasted marrow and crispy bacon on a plate. Season with salt and pepper. Optionally, garnish with parsley or a squeeze of lemon for extra flavor.

Macronutrient Breakdown:

Fat: 80% | **Protein:** 18% | **Carbs:** 2% (trace amounts)

Ingredients:

- 200 g (7 oz) bacon (thin strips)
- 2 bone marrow bones (cut in half)
- Salt and pepper to taste

GRILLED RED MULLET WITH GARLIC BUTTER

Instructions:

- Clean the red mullets and season them with salt.
- Melt the butter in a pan over low heat, then add the minced garlic. Cook for 1 minute until fragrant.
- Preheat the grill or a skillet over medium-high heat.
- Cook the red mullets for about 4 minutes per side until golden and crispy.
- Drizzle the garlic butter over the fish before serving.

Macronutrient Breakdown:

Fats: 70% | **Proteins:** 30% | **Carb.:** 0%

Ingredients:

- 2 fresh red mullets
- 2 tbsp butter
- 1 garlic clove, minced
- Salt to taste

BUTTER LAMB STEW

Instructions:

- **Brown the Lamb:** Heat butter and olive oil in a large pot over medium-high heat. Add the lamb and sear until browned on all sides. Remove and set aside.
- **Sauté Vegetables:** In the same pot, add onion and garlic. Cook for 3-4 minutes until fragrant.
- **Simmer:** Return lamb to the pot, add broth, rosemary, cumin, salt, and pepper. Cover and cook on low heat for 45 minutes, stirring occasionally.
- **Add Mushrooms & Spinach:** Stir in mushrooms and cook for 10 minutes. Then, add spinach and cook until wilted (2-3 minutes).
- **Optional Creamy Touch:** Stir in heavy cream for a richer texture.

Ingredients:

- 400 g lamb
- 2 tbsp unsalted butter
- 1 tbsp extra virgin olive oil
- 1 small onion, finely chopped
- 2 garlic cloves, minced
- 1 cup bone broth (lamb or chicken)
- 100 g mushrooms, sliced
- 100 g fresh spinach
- 1 tsp dried or fresh rosemary
- ½ tsp ground cumin
- Salt and black pepper to taste

Macronutrient Breakdown:

Fats: 70% | **Proteins:** 25% | **Carbs:** 5%

Day 24: Luxury Meats to Celebrate

Motivation: Enjoy premium cuts as part of your carnivore consolidation.

Meal Plan:

- **Breakfast:** Omelet with cheese and bacon.
- **Lunch:** Grilled Wagyu with butter.
- **Dinner:** Oven-roasted lamb leg with herbs.

Ingredients (2 servings):
- 2 large eggs
- 100g beef or chicken liver (chicken liver has a milder taste)
- 50g shredded cheese (cheddar, gouda, or mozzarella)
- ¼ small onion (optional, finely chopped)
- 1 garlic clove (minced)
- 2 tbsp butter or coconut oil
- Salt and pepper to taste
- Fresh herbs (parsley or cilantro, optional, for garnish)

OMELETTE WITH CHEESE AND BACON

Instructions:

- **Prepare the liver:** Remove any membranes or tough tissues. Cut into small pieces and season with salt and pepper.
- **Cook the liver:** In a pan, melt 1 tbsp butter over medium heat. Sauté garlic and onion until translucent. Add the liver and cook for 3-4 minutes until browned and fully cooked. Set aside.
- **Beat the eggs:** In a bowl, whisk eggs with a pinch of salt and pepper.
- **Cook the omelette:** In the same pan, melt the remaining butter. Pour in the eggs and cook for 1-2 minutes until they begin to set.
- **Fill the omelette:** Add the cooked liver and cheese to one side. Fold over and cook for 1 more minute until the cheese melts.
- **Serve:** Transfer to a plate and garnish with fresh herbs if desired.

Macronutrient Ratio:

Fat: 70% | **Protein:** 25% | **Carbs:** 5%

WAGYU STEAK ON THE GRILL

Instructions:

- Heat a skillet over high heat until very hot.
- Season the Wagyu steak generously with sea salt.
- Sear the steak for 2-3 minutes per side, depending on thickness, to achieve a medium-rare doneness.
- Add clarified butter to the skillet in the final minute, basting the steak for extra richness.
- Remove from heat and let it rest for 5 minutes before serving to retain its juices.

Ingredients:
- 200 g Wagyu steak
- 1 tbsp clarified butter
- Sea salt to taste

Macronutrient Breakdown (Approximate per serving):

Fat: 70% | **Protein:** 30% | **Carbs:** 0%

HERB-ROASTED LAMB LEG

Instructions:

- Prepare the Lamb: Preheat oven to 180°C (350°F). Pat dry the lamb and make small cuts on the surface for better absorption of flavors.
- Marinate: Mix garlic, rosemary, thyme, olive oil, lemon juice, salt, and pepper in a bowl. Rub generously over the lamb pieces.
- Roast: Place lamb in a baking dish. Pour wine or broth into the dish for added moisture. Cover with foil and bake for 45-50 minutes, turning halfway through.
- Crisp the Surface: Remove foil in the last 15 minutes for a golden crust.
- Rest and Serve: Let the lamb rest for 5-10 minutes before slicing.

Ingredients:
- 2 lamb leg pieces (300-350 g each)
- 2 garlic cloves, minced
- 1 sprig fresh rosemary
- 1 sprig fresh thyme
- 2 tbsp extra virgin olive oil
- Juice of ½ lemon
- ½ tsp sea salt
- ¼ tsp black pepper
- ¼ cup dry white wine or chicken broth

Macronutrient Breakdown (per serving):

Fat: 70% | **Protein:** 28% | **Carbs:** 2%

Day 25: Complex Cuts with Advanced Techniques

Motivation: Learn how to prepare large cuts to share or store as leftovers.

Meal Plan:

- **Breakfast:** Scrambled eggs with duck fat.
- **Lunch:** Smoked brisket.
- **Dinner:** Braised beef tongue.

SCRAMBLED EGGS WITH DUCK FAT (2 SERVINGS)

Instructions:

- Lightly beat the eggs in a bowl.
- Heat the duck fat in a skillet over medium-low heat.
- Pour the eggs into the pan and let them sit for a few seconds.
- Gently stir with a spatula, forming soft folds.
- Season with salt and pepper to taste.
- Remove from heat when creamy and slightly set.
- Serve immediately.

Ingredients:

- 4 eggs
- 1 tbsp duck fat
- Salt and pepper to taste
- **Optional:** fresh herbs (parsley or chives)

Macronutrient Breakdown:

Fat: 75% | **Protein:** 23% | **Carbohydrates:** 2%

SMOKED BRISKET

Instructions:

- Generously season the brisket with coarse salt and black pepper.
- Preheat the smoker to 120°C (250°F). Place the brisket fat-side up.
- Smoke for 6-8 hours, or until the internal temperature reaches 93°C (200°F).
- Remove from the smoker and let it rest for 30 minutes before slicing thinly.
- **Alternative method:** If you don't have a smoker, wrap the brisket in aluminum foil, bake at 120°C (250°F) for 6-8 hours, and add a few drops of liquid smoke for flavor.

Ingredients:

- 1.5 kg (3.3 lbs) beef brisket
- Coarse salt
- Black pepper

Macronutrient Breakdown (per 100g):

Fat: 70% | **Protein:** 30% | **Carbs:** 0%

BEEF TONGUE STEW

Instructions:

- **Prepare the Tongue:** Rinse under cold water. Boil in salted water for 20 minutes. Remove, let cool, and peel off the thick skin.
- **Sauté the Vegetables:** Heat olive oil in a large pot. Sauté onions, garlic, carrots, and celery for 5-7 min.
- **Brown the Tongue:** Slice into thick pieces. Add to the pot and brown both sides.
- **Make the Stew:** Add crushed tomatoes, bay leaves, and thyme. Cook for 5 minutes. Pour in red wine (if using) and reduce for 3-4 minutes.
- **Simmer:** Add broth, season with salt and pepper, cover, and cook on low for 1.5-2 hours until tender.
- **Serve:** Enjoy with cauliflower mash or steamed veggies.

Ingredients:

- 1 beef tongue
- 2 medium onions
- 3 garlic cloves
- 2 carrots
- 1 celery stalk
- 2 bay leaves
- 1 sprig of fresh thyme
- 1 cup crushed tomatoes
- 1/2 cup red wine
- 3 cups beef broth or water
- 2 tbsp olive oil
- Salt and pepper to taste

Macronutrient Breakdown (per serving):

Fat: 70% | **Protein:** 25% | **Carbs:** 5%

Day 26: Sophisticated Dishes for the Refined Palate

Motivation: Introduce elaborate preparations that showcase how versatile this lifestyle can be.

Meal Plan:

- **Breakfast:** Roasted bone marrow with poached egg.
- **Lunch:** Minted lamb ribs.
- **Dinner:** Ribeye steak with herb butter.

Ingredients:
- 2 bone marrow bones (5-7 cm long)
- 2 eggs
- 1 tbsp white vinegar
- Salt and pepper to taste
- Fresh parsley, chopped (optional)

ROASTED BONE MARROW WITH POACHED EGG

Instructions:

- **Roast the Bone Marrow:** Preheat the oven to 220°C (425°F). Place the bones on a baking tray, cut side up. Season with salt and pepper. Roast for 15-20 minutes until the marrow is soft and slightly bubbling.

- **Poach the Eggs:** Heat water in a saucepan with vinegar until it simmers. Create a whirlpool with a spoon and gently drop in one egg. Cook for 3-4 minutes, then remove with a slotted spoon. Repeat for the second egg.

- **Serve:** Place the roasted marrow bones on a plate. Top each with a poached egg. Garnish with fresh parsley and additional seasoning to taste.

Macronutrient Breakdown:

Fat: 75% | **Protein:** 23% | **Carbohydrates:** 2%

RIBEYE STEAK WITH HERB BUTTER

Instructions:
- Heat a skillet over high heat.
- Sear the ribeye for 3-4 minutes per side for medium-rare or until desired doneness.
- In a small pan, melt the butter over low heat and mix in the herbs.
- Let the steak rest for 5 minutes, then pour the herb butter over it before serving.
- **Tip:** Serve with bone broth for a more nutritious meal.

Macronutrient Ratio:
Fat: 70% | Protein: 30% | Carbs: 0%

Ingredients:
- 250 g (8.8 oz) ribeye steak
- 2 tbsp butter
- 1 tsp mixed herbs (rosemary, thyme)

MINT-INFUSED LAMB RACK

Instructions:
- **Prepare the Lamb:** Trim excess fat and membrane. If preferred, clean the bones for a "frenched rack" presentation.
- **Make the Marinade:** Mix garlic, mint, rosemary, thyme, lemon zest, olive oil, mustard, honey, salt, and pepper.
- **Marinate:** Coat the lamb with the mixture, ensuring even coverage. Refrigerate for at least 2 hours (overnight for deeper flavor).
- **Sear:** Heat a pan over medium-high heat. Sear the lamb for 2-3 minutes per side until golden.
- **Roast:** Preheat oven to 200°C (390°F). Place lamb in a baking tray, bone-side down. Roast for 15-20 minutes for medium doneness (55-60°C or 130-140°F internal temperature).
- **Rest:** Remove from oven, cover with foil, and let rest for 10 minutes.
- **Serve:** Slice into portions and garnish with fresh mint.

Macronutrient Breakdown:
Fat: 70% | Protein: 28% | Carbs: 2% (from honey and mustard)

Ingredients:
- 1 kg lamb rack
- 2 garlic cloves, finely chopped
- 2 tbsp fresh mint, chopped
- 1 tbsp fresh rosemary, chopped
- 1 tsp dried thyme (optional)
- Zest of 1 lemon
- 3 tbsp extra virgin olive oil
- 1 tbsp Dijon mustard
- 1 tbsp honey
- Salt and pepper to taste

Day 27: Complete Preparations

Motivation: Master recipes that require time and technique to enjoy a true carnivore feast.

Meal Plan:

- **Breakfast:** Eggs with beef liver.
- **Lunch:** Roasted suckling pig.
- **Dinner:** Braised oxtail.

BEEF LIVER AND EGGS

Instructions:

- **Prepare the Liver:** Rinse the beef liver under cold water and pat dry. Remove any white membrane or excess fat. Cut into small pieces for even cooking.

- **Sauté the Liver:** Heat a skillet over medium heat and melt the butter. Add the garlic and onion, cooking until soft and translucent. Add the liver pieces, season with salt and pepper, and cook for 3-4 minutes per side. Remove from the skillet and set aside.

- **Cook the Eggs:** In the same skillet, crack the eggs and cook them to your preference. Return the liver to the pan to reheat slightly.

- **Serve:** Plate the eggs with the warm liver. Optionally, garnish with fresh parsley or cilantro.

Ingredients:
- 150 g beef liver
- 2 large eggs
- 1/4 onion, finely chopped
- 1 garlic clove, minced
- 1 tbsp butter
- Salt and pepper to taste

Macronutrient Breakdown:

Fat: 60% | **Protein:** 38% | **Carbs:** 2%

BRAISED OXTAIL (CARNIVORE DIET RECIPE)

Instructions:

- **Sear the Oxtail:** Heat a heavy-bottomed pot over medium-high heat. Sear the oxtail on all sides until browned.

- **Slow Cook:** Pour in the bone broth, reduce the heat to low, and cover the pot. Let it simmer for 4-5 hours, or until the meat is fall-off-the-bone tender.

- **Serve:** Plate the oxtail with its natural juices. Enjoy warm.

Ingredients:
- 800 g (1.76 lbs) oxtail
- 2 cups bone broth
- Salt and garlic powder to taste

Macronutrient Breakdown (Approximate):

Fat: 70% | **Protein:** 30% | **Carbs:** 0%

ROAST SUCKLING PIG (CARNIVORE STYLE)

Instructions:

- **Prepare the Pig:** Pat the pig dry with paper towels. Score the skin lightly to prevent curling. Rub coarse salt inside and out. Optionally, marinate overnight with minced garlic, herbs, and a drizzle of olive oil.

- **Slow Roasting:** Preheat oven to 150°C (300°F). Place the pig skin-side up on a rack over a roasting pan with a little water. Roast for 2 hours to keep the meat tender.

- **Crisping the Skin:** Increase oven temperature to 200°C (400°F). Brush the skin with pork lard or olive oil. Roast for another 30-45 minutes until golden and crispy. Watch carefully to avoid burning.

- **Rest & Serve:** Let the pig rest for 10 minutes before carving.

Ingredients:
- 1/2 suckling pig (about 3 kg)
- 2-3 garlic cloves, minced
- Coarse salt
- Ground black pepper
- Pork lard (optional, for extra crispiness)
- **Optional:** thyme, rosemary, or bay leaves

Macronutrient Breakdown:

Fat: 75% | **Protein:** 25% | **Carbs:** 0%

Day 28: Finish with Excellence

> Motivation: Celebrate your success with a carnivore feast that highlights everything you've learned.

Meal Plan:

- **Breakfast:** Cheese and bone marrow omelet.
- **Lunch:** Grilled T-bone steak.
- **Dinner:** Pork leg with a butter crust.

CHEESE & BONE MARROW OMELETTE

Ingredients:
- 4 eggs
- 100 g bone marrow
- 50 g shredded cheese (mozzarella or cheddar)
- 1 tbsp butter or olive oil
- Salt and pepper to taste

Instructions:
- Heat butter in a pan over medium heat. Add bone marrow and cook until lightly browned.
- In a bowl, whisk eggs with salt and pepper. Pour over the marrow.
- Sprinkle shredded cheese on top. Cook on low heat until set.
- Fold the omelette in half and cook for another minute.
- Serve hot, garnished with fresh herbs if desired.

Macronutrient Breakdown:
Fat: 75% | **Protein**: 25% | **Carbohydrates**: 0%

CRISPY PORK LEG WITH LARD CRUST

Instructions:

- Preheat the oven to 200°C (400°F).
- **Prepare the pork:** Pat dry the pork leg. Rub it generously with lard, ensuring full coverage. Sprinkle coarse salt evenly.
- **Roast:** Place the pork leg in a roasting pan and cook for 2 hours, basting occasionally with its own fat.
- **Crisp the crust:** Increase the temperature to 220°C (430°F) for the last 20 minutes to achieve a crispy, golden-brown crust.
- **Rest and serve:** Remove from the oven and let it rest for 10 minutes before slicing. Enjoy with your favorite low-carb side dish.

Ingredients:

- 1.5 kg (3.3 lbs) pork leg
- 3 tbsp lard
- Coarse salt to taste

Macronutrient Breakdown (per 100g):

Fat: 70% | **Protein:** 30% | **Carbs:** 0%

GRILLED T-BONE STEAK

Instructions:

- **Prepare the Steak:** Remove the T-bone from the fridge 30 minutes before cooking. Pat it dry with paper towels and season generously with salt and pepper. Optionally, rub with olive oil or butter for extra flavor.
- **Preheat the Grill:** Heat the grill to high. If using charcoal, wait until the coals are white-hot.
- **Sear the Steak:** Place the T-bone directly over the heat. Sear for 2-3 minutes per side to get grill marks.
- **Cook to Desired Doneness:** Move the steak to indirect heat and cook until reaching the desired internal temperature:
    - Rare: 125°F (52°C)
    - Medium Rare: 135°F (57°C)
    - Medium: 145°F (63°C)
    - Well Done: 160°F (71°C)
- Rest and Serve: Let the steak rest for 5-10 minutes before slicing.

Ingredients:

- 1 T-bone steak (14-18 oz)
- Coarse salt
- Freshly ground black pepper
- Olive oil or melted butter (optional)
- Fresh herbs (rosemary or thyme, optional)

Macronutrient Breakdown (Per Serving):

Fat: 70% | **Protein:** 30% | **Carbs:** 0%

28-Day Carnivore Challenge Meal Plan

This table provides a detailed meal plan for each day of the 28-Day Carnivore Challenge, organized into breakfast, lunch, and dinner. It is designed to make your transition to the carnivore lifestyle easier, ensuring variety, optimal nutrition, and simplicity in meal preparation.

How to Use This Table?

Follow the daily plan: Each day includes three complete meals with the right balance of protein and healthy fats. This eliminates the need for meal planning.

Explore variety: Throughout the 28 days, you'll try different cuts of meat, organ meats, and cooking methods that maximize nutrition.

Adjust to your needs: If a recipe includes a cut or ingredient you don't like, you can substitute it with a similar option while keeping the focus on animal-based foods.

Build lasting habits: This plan not only guides you through the challenge but also teaches you how to structure your meals in a simple and effective way, so you can maintain this lifestyle beyond the 28 days.

Day	Breakfast	Lunch	Dinner
Day 1	Scrambled eggs with butter	Beef burger with cheese and bacon	Grilled chicken breast
Day 2	Cheese omelet	Grilled pork chop	Butter-herb salmon
Day 3	Fried eggs in pork lard	Beef meatballs in their own juices	Ribeye steak with garlic butter
Day 4	Boiled eggs and bacon	Oven-baked pork ribs	Pan-seared white fish fillet
Day 5	Poached eggs with melted butter	Crispy skin baked chicken thighs	Pork loin cooked in lard
Day 6	Crispy bacon with fried egg	Additive-free pork sausages	Oven-baked beef ribs
Day 7	Omelet with chicken liver and bacon	Grilled beef steak with bone marrow	Pork chop with garlic butter

Day 8	Sautéed beef liver with butter	Slow-cooked pork ribs	Baked fish fillet with herbs
Day 9	Fried eggs with bone marrow	Stewed beef heart	Roasted pork tongue
Day 10	Fried eggs in butter	Oven-roasted beef	Grilled pork chops
Day 11	Scrambled eggs with duck fat	Braised pork feet	Stewed pork trotters
Day 12	Eggs with beef liver	Stewed beef tongue	Oxtail stew
Day 13	Eggs with duck liver	Sautéed brains with butter	Roasted beef tongue
Day 14	Pancetta with bone marrow	Stewed pork ears	Beef tongue with bone marrow
Day 15	Eggs Benedict with butter	Prime rib roast	Marrow-infused lamb chops
Day 16	Crispy bacon with bone marrow	Lamb stew with butter	Braised lamb with garlic
Day 17	Omelet with cheese and pancetta	Grilled Wagyu steak	Roasted pork leg
Day 18	Scrambled eggs with duck fat	Smoked beef brisket	Leg of lamb with garlic
Day 19	Eggs with liver and cheese	Lamb ribs with mint	Oxtail stew
Day 20	Roasted bone marrow with poached egg	Oven-roasted suckling pig	Oven-roasted pork leg
Day 21	Scrambled eggs with butter	T-bone steak	Lamb leg
Day 22	Fried eggs in pork lard	Beef tongue stew	Beef bone broth with tongue
Day 23	Boiled eggs with butter	Grilled red mullet	Braised oxtail stew
Day 24	Bacon and fried egg	Sautéed kidneys	Oven-roasted ribs
Day 25	Fried eggs with pork fat	Braised lamb shank	Braised pork knuckle
Day 26	Poached eggs with bone marrow	Grilled pork chop	Lamb tongue stew
Day 27	Cheese omelet	Lamb leg roast	Marinated pork ribs
Day 28	Eggs with bone marrow	Marinated pork chops	Oven-roasted lamb leg

Cocktails, Juices, and Smoothies

To accompany your delicious carnivore recipes, we present a selection of 16 drinks, including cocktails, juices, and smoothies, that will enhance every bite. From refreshing mojitos to nutritious smoothies, these drinks are designed to complement the bold flavors of your meat dishes and make every meal a memorable experience. Cheers and enjoy!

Cocktails

Strawberry Mojito

- **Ingredients**: White rum, strawberries, mint, sugar, lime juice, soda water, ice.
- **Instructions:** Muddle the strawberries and mint with sugar and lime juice. Add the rum and ice, then top with soda water.

Passion Fruit Caipiroska

- **Ingredients:** Vodka, passion fruit, sugar, ice.
- **Instructions:** Mix the passion fruit pulp with sugar. Add the vodka and ice, and mix well.

Piña Colada

- **Ingredients:** Rum, coconut cream, pineapple juice, ice.
- **Instructions:** Blend all ingredients until smooth.

Mango Margarita

- **Ingredients:** Tequila, orange liqueur, mango juice, lime juice, ice.
- **Instructions:** Mix all ingredients in a shaker with ice and shake well.

Juices

Green Detox Juice

- Ingredients: Spinach, cucumber, green apple, ginger, lime, water.
- Instructions: Blend all ingredients until smooth. Strain if necessary.

Orange and Carrot Juice

- Ingredients: Oranges, carrots, ginger.
- Instructions: Extract the juice from the oranges and carrots. Add some grated ginger and mix well.

Berry Juice

- Ingredients: Strawberries, raspberries, blueberries, lime juice, water.
- Instructions: Blend all ingredients with a little water until smooth. Strain if necessary.

Watermelon and Mint Juice

- Ingredients: Watermelon, mint leaves, lime juice.
- Instructions: Blend the watermelon and mint leaves. Add lime juice and mix well.

Smoothies

Banana and Oat Smoothie

- Ingredients: Bananas, oats, milk, honey, cinnamon.
- Instructions: Blend all ingredients until smooth and homogeneous.

Strawberry and Banana Smoothie

- Ingredients: Strawberries, banana, plain yogurt, milk, honey.
- Instructions: Blend all ingredients until smooth.

Tropical Smoothie

- Ingredients: Mango, pineapple, coconut milk, orange juice.
- Instructions: Blend all ingredients until smooth.

Chocolate and Coffee Smoothie

- Ingredients: Milk, cocoa powder, espresso coffee, vanilla ice cream.
- Instructions: Blend all ingredients until creamy.

Green Smoothies

Spinach and Apple Smoothie
- **Ingredients:** Spinach, green apple, lime juice, water, ice.
- **Instructions:** Blend all ingredients until smooth.

Kale and Pineapple Smoothie
- **Ingredients:** Kale, pineapple, almond milk, banana.
- **Instructions:** Blend all ingredients until smooth.

Refreshing Drinks

Coconut Lemonade
- **Ingredients:** Lemon juice, coconut water, sugar, ice.
- **Instructions:** Mix all ingredients until the sugar is completely dissolved.

Cucumber and Lemon Water
- **Ingredients:** Cucumber, lemon, mint leaves, water.
- **Instructions:** Slice the cucumber and lemon, and mix with water and mint leaves. Refrigerate and serve with ice.

Conclusion and Next Steps

Benefits Achieved in 28 Days

By completing this 28-Day Carnivore Challenge, you have likely experienced a series of transformations in your body and overall well-being. Here is a summary of the most significant benefits you may have noticed during this time:

Improved Energy Levels

One of the first benefits of adopting a carnivore diet is the increase in energy levels. During the first few weeks, your body has learned to use fat as its primary energy source, allowing you to enjoy more stable and sustained energy throughout the day. As your body adapts, you will notice that you no longer experience the energy spikes and crashes associated with carbohydrates.

Weight Loss and Improved Body Composition

The carnivore diet is naturally low in carbohydrates, which helps reduce insulin levels and facilitates fat burning. Over these 28 days, you have likely lost weight, especially abdominal fat, and noticed an improvement in muscle tone due to higher protein and healthy fat intake.

Reduced Inflammation

By eliminating processed foods, sugars, and refined carbohydrates, you have significantly reduced factors that contribute to chronic inflammation. Many people report noticeable improvements in conditions such as arthritis, joint pain, and other inflammation-related ailments.

Improved Mental Health and Cognitive Clarity

The carnivore diet, being rich in healthy fats and essential nutrients, provides the necessary components for brain health. As a result, it is common to experience greater mental clarity, improved focus, and reduced anxiety. Many people also report enhanced mood and overall well-being.

Optimized Digestive Health

The carnivore diet eliminates foods that can cause digestive issues, such as grains, legumes, and vegetables high in insoluble fiber. As a result, you have likely experienced improved digestion, reduced bloating and gas, and more regular bowel movements.

Improved Cholesterol Levels and Cardiovascular Health

Although high saturated fat intake was once feared to raise cholesterol and cause heart disease, many people following the carnivore diet have experienced improvements in their cholesterol levels, with increased HDL (the 'good' cholesterol) and reduced LDL and triglycerides. This contributes to better cardiovascular health.

How to Continue the Carnivore Diet

At the end of the 28-day challenge, you have the option to continue with the carnivore diet or make adjustments based on your personal goals. Here are some options to maintain or modify your carnivore lifestyle in a sustainable way:

Full Carnivore Diet Maintenance

If you have felt great during the challenge and want to continue reaping the benefits of the carnivore diet, you can maintain it as your lifestyle. To do so, make sure to follow these principles:

- **Eat Quality Meat:** Continue choosing fresh, organic meat whenever possible. Include a variety of meats (beef, pork, chicken, fish, and seafood) and don't forget nutrient-rich organs (liver, kidneys, etc.).

- **Include Healthy Fats:** Don't hesitate to consume animal fats such as pork lard, tallow, butter, and duck fat. These fats are essential for energy and hormonal health.

- **Keep It Simple:** The carnivore diet is easy to follow because it is based on eating whole, unprocessed foods. Avoid products that contain sugars, refined carbohydrates, or artificial ingredients.

- **Listen to Your Body:** While the carnivore diet is powerful, each person is different. Pay attention to your body's signals and adjust your meat and fat portions based on your energy needs.

Gradual Introduction of Some Foods

If you feel you have achieved your goals but do not want to remain fully carnivore, you can start reintroducing some foods gradually:

- **Low-Carb Vegetables:** Consider incorporating small amounts of low-carb vegetables such as spinach, broccoli, zucchini, and cucumber. Ensure these foods complement your meals rather than become the main focus.

- **Nuts and Seeds:** If you want to add variety to your diet, nuts and seeds can be a healthy option, as long as they do not contain added sugars.

- **High-Quality Dairy:** Whole dairy products from grass-fed animals (such as cheese, yogurt, or cream) can be a good addition for those who tolerate dairy well. Opt for unsweetened and unprocessed versions.

Carnivore Diet Cycling

If you prefer a more flexible approach, you can adopt a 'cycling' strategy with the carnivore diet. This means following a strict carnivore diet for certain periods of the week (e.g., 4-5 days) and then incorporating 2-3 days of additional foods such as low-carb vegetables, some dairy, or fruits. This approach allows you to maintain the benefits of the carnivore diet while introducing some variety.

Monitoring and Adjustments

After completing the 28 days, it is important to continue monitoring how you feel. Consider doing periodic health check-ups (e.g., blood tests to monitor cholesterol and other indicators) and adjust your diet as needed. Many people find that as their health improves, they can reduce their intake of processed meats or vary the cuts they consume depending on their needs.

Final Conclusion

Congratulations on completing the 28-Day Carnivore Challenge! Over these weeks, you have experienced a transformation in your physical and mental health and have taken an important step towards improving your well-being. Remember that this lifestyle can be as flexible as you want, and you can adapt it to your long-term goals. Whether you decide to continue with the carnivore diet or make adjustments to incorporate more foods, the most important thing is to listen to your body, maintain healthy habits, and enjoy the benefits you have achieved.

Now, with the knowledge and tools you have gained, you are ready to continue living a healthy and fulfilling life. Wishing you continued success and good health on your carnivore journey!

Made in the USA
Monee, IL
21 August 2025

23923687R00056